The
Vintage Coloring Book

Old San Francisco and Early California

Written and Illustrated
by Carol Hill

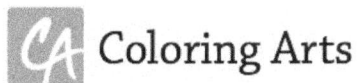
CA Coloring Arts

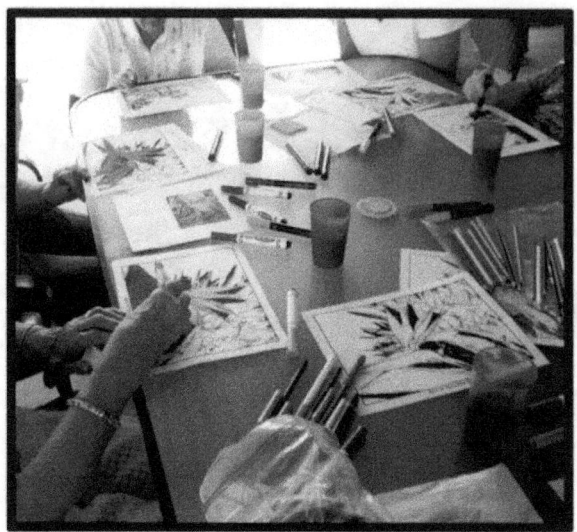

Thanks to the residents of the retirement homes who colored many of these pictures and helped with the selection of the pictures featured in these books. Also, thanks to the online Wikipedia for its many facts that helped with the writing of this book.

A special thanks to those who gave permission to use their colored pictures on the cover.

For more product information visit www.coloringarts.com

The Value of Coloring

by Dr. Victoria Anderson, Ph.D.

There are therapeutic effects to coloring. It engages the right side of the brain, stimulating relaxing and pleasurable effects. It can be most helpful for senior participants for several reasons:

1. Coloring can bring back past childhood memories with positive emotional effects.

2. Coloring can improve hand-eye coordination.

3. Coloring can be a social activity which stimulates verbal interactions with other participants.

4. Coloring may also help with focus and concentration.

5. Coloring often brings a sense of accomplishment and feelings of completion.

6. Coloring is fun for all ages!

Music Pavillion in Golden Gate Park
"Temple of Music"

The Temple of Music in Golden Gate Park was built on the Music Concourse in 1900. It was a gift to the city of San Francisco from Charles Spreckels, the "Sugar King." Even today, the Golden Gate Park Band is still giving free concerts there every weekend.

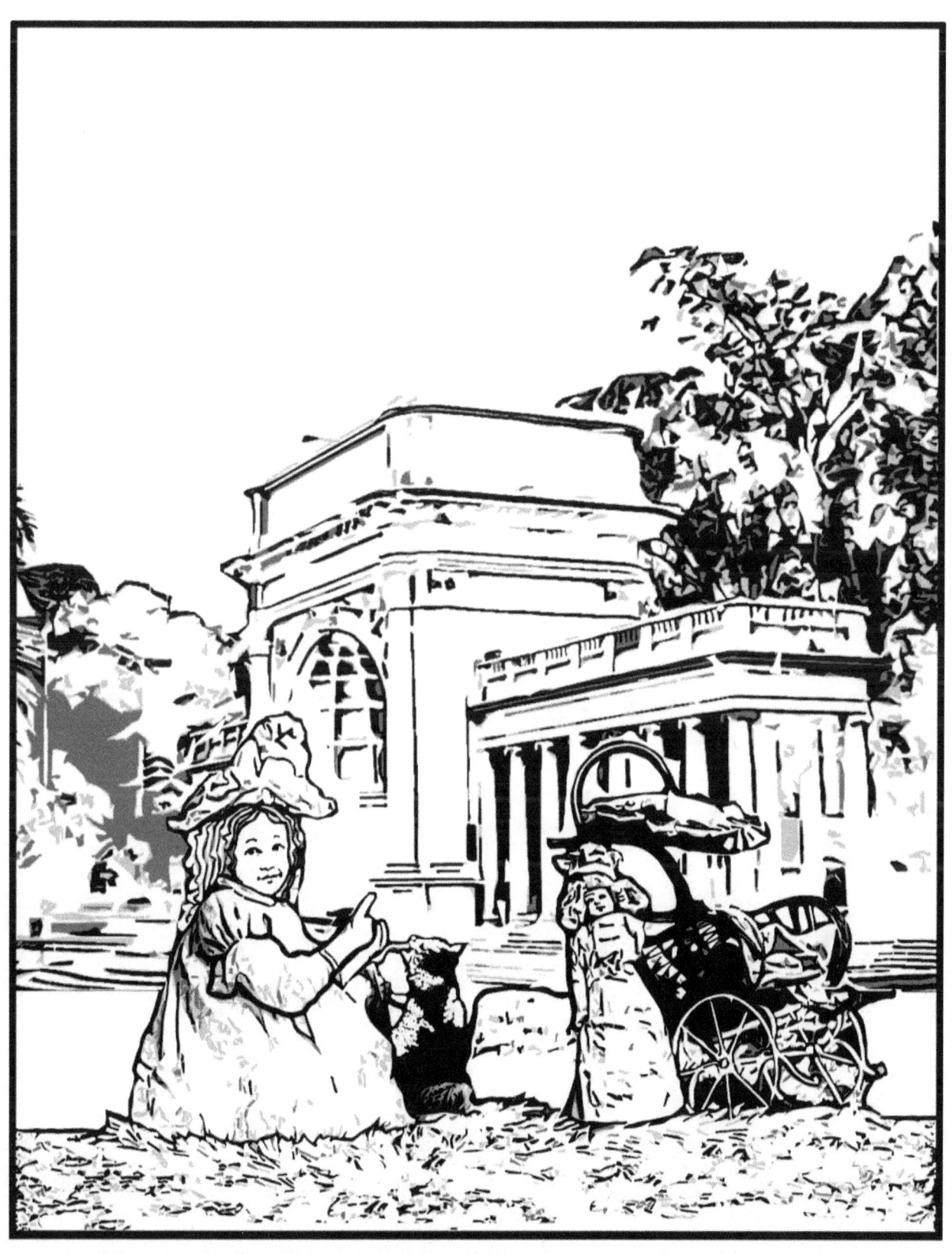

The Music Pavillion in Golden Gate Park, San Francisco - 1915

1906 - Year of the San Francisco Earthquake

Many families lost their homes and possessions during the terrible earthquake and fire that ravaged most of San Francisco in 1906. Thousands became homeless overnight, and many buildings were destroyed or greatly damaged.

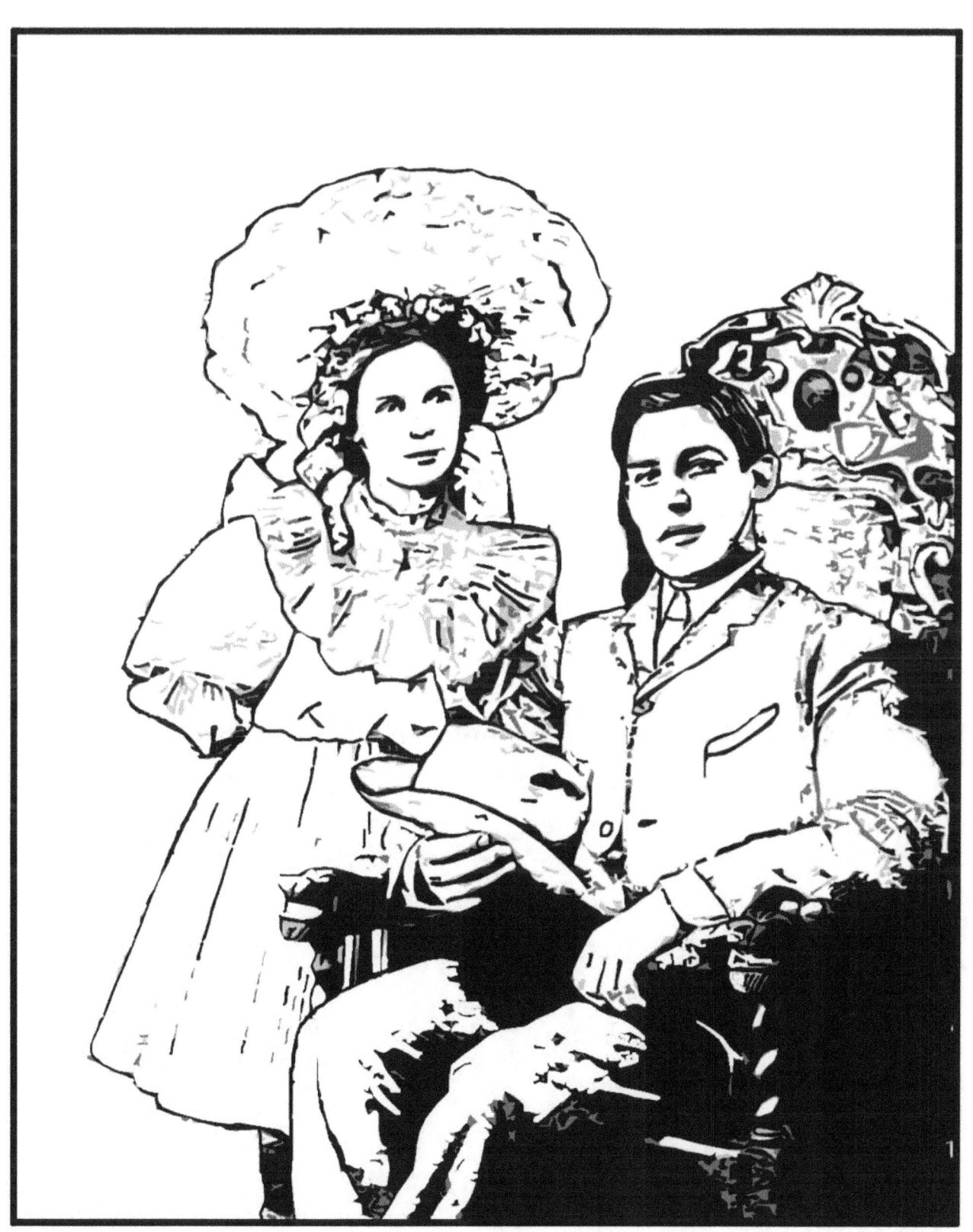

A Family Portrait - 1906

San Francisco Mint

The San Francisco Mint was one of the few buildings
that escaped real damage during the earthquake of 1906.
The original Mint was built in 1854, with the approval and
recommendation of President Fillmore.

There were large amounts of gold coming out of California
during the gold rush. The gold needed to be minted into coins,
and it became necessary to establish a Mint in California.

The first building was soon replaced with this larger one,
resembling a Greek temple. The Mint remained there
until 1937 when it moved to a modern, larger building.

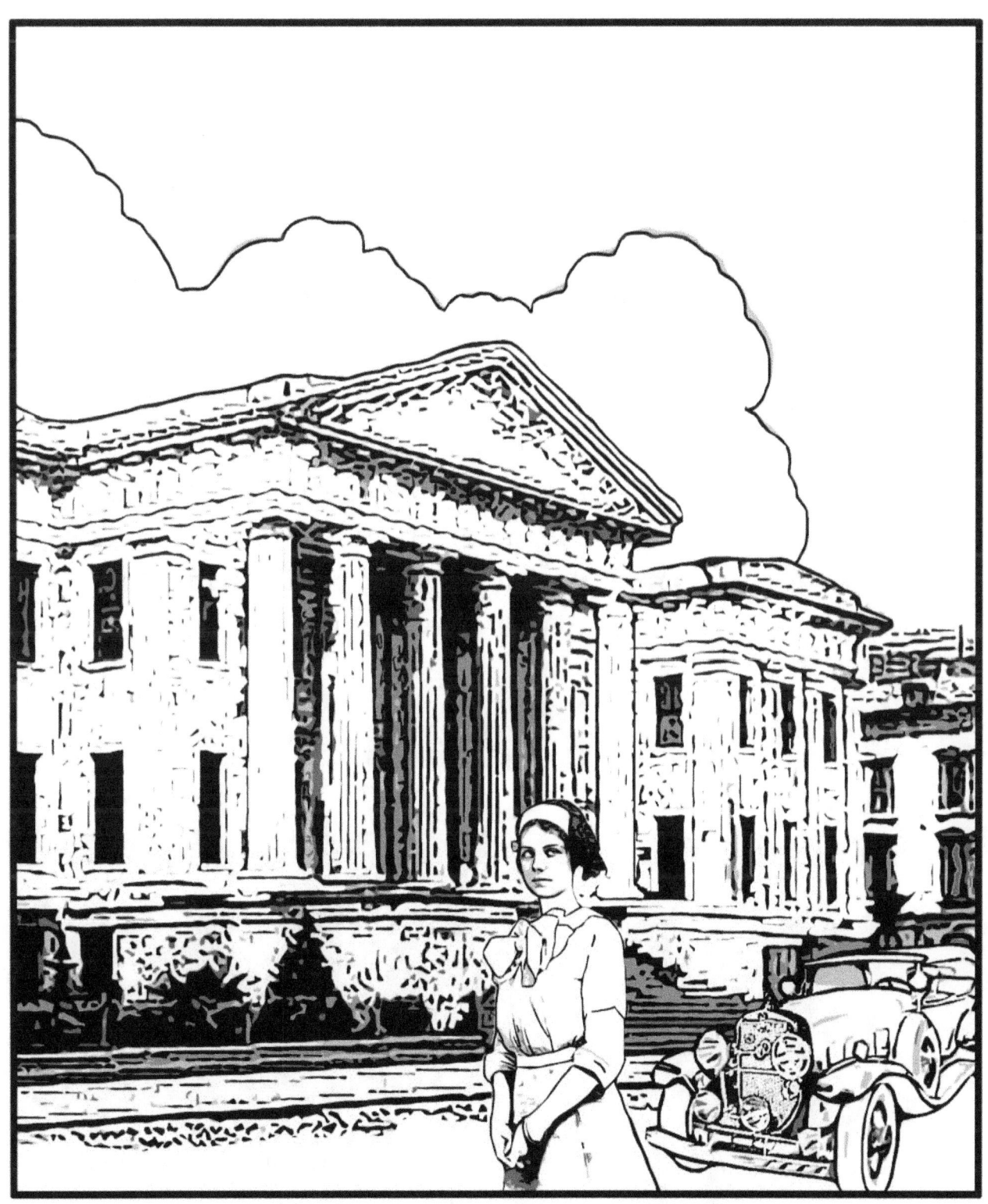

The San Francisco Mint - abt 1910

Conservatory of Flowers

The Conservatory of Flowers is the oldest building in Golden Gate Park. It was completed in 1878. It is the oldest conservatory on the Western hemisphere. It was designed after the victorian style buildings of its era. It houses rare tropical flowers, plants, and trees from all over the world.

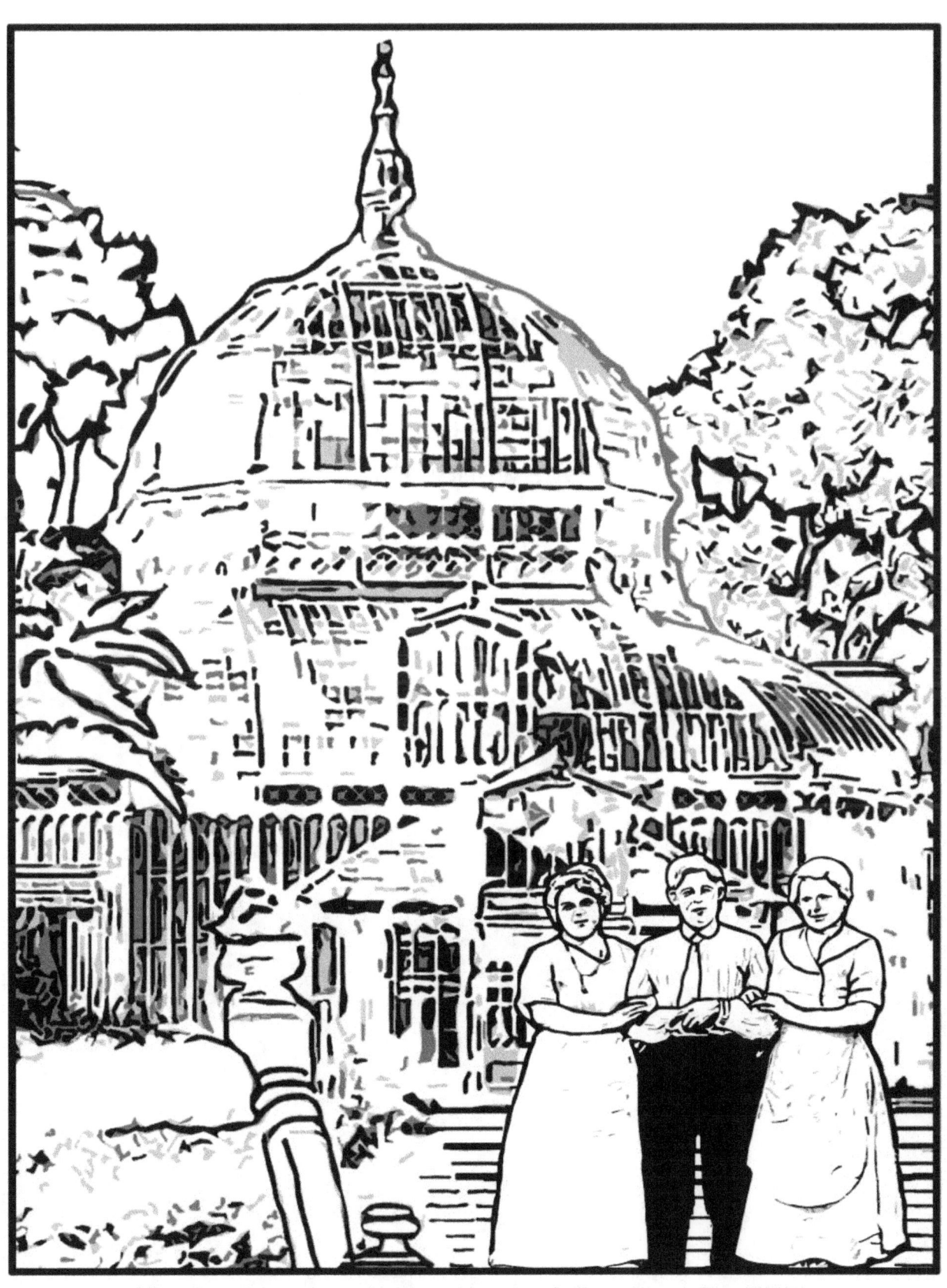

The San Francisco Conservatory of Flowers - abt. 1890

Conservatory of Flowers - Orchid Collection

The orchid collection in the Conservatory is one of the largest collections in the world. It houses more than 700 species of orchids - there are only about 1,000 known species in the world.

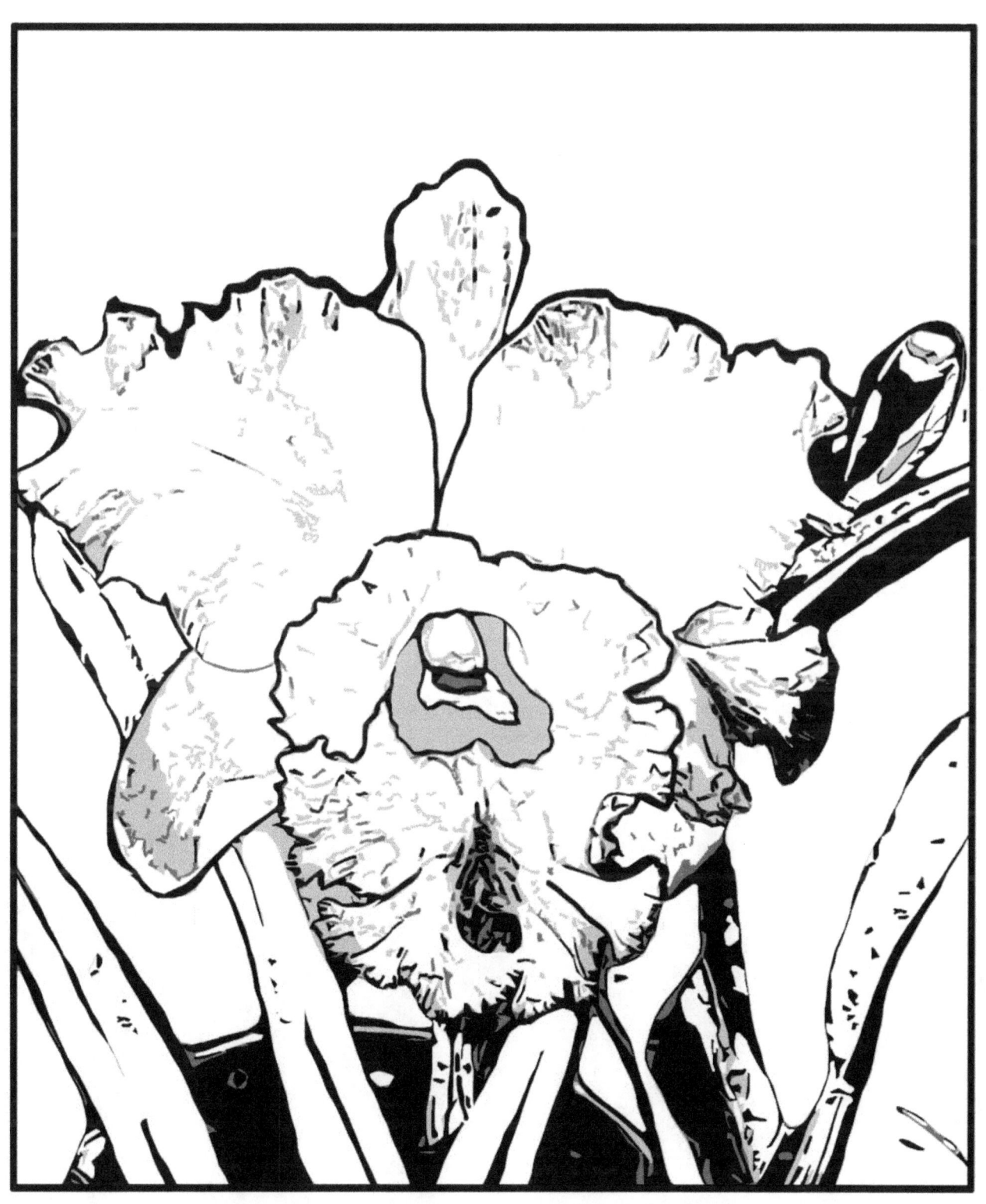

Rare Tropical Orchids

Many Rare Plants in the Conservatory

The Conservatory of Flowers houses about 1,700 different plant species. They include the lowland plants, the highland plants, aquatic plants, carnivorous plants, and potted plants of all varieties.

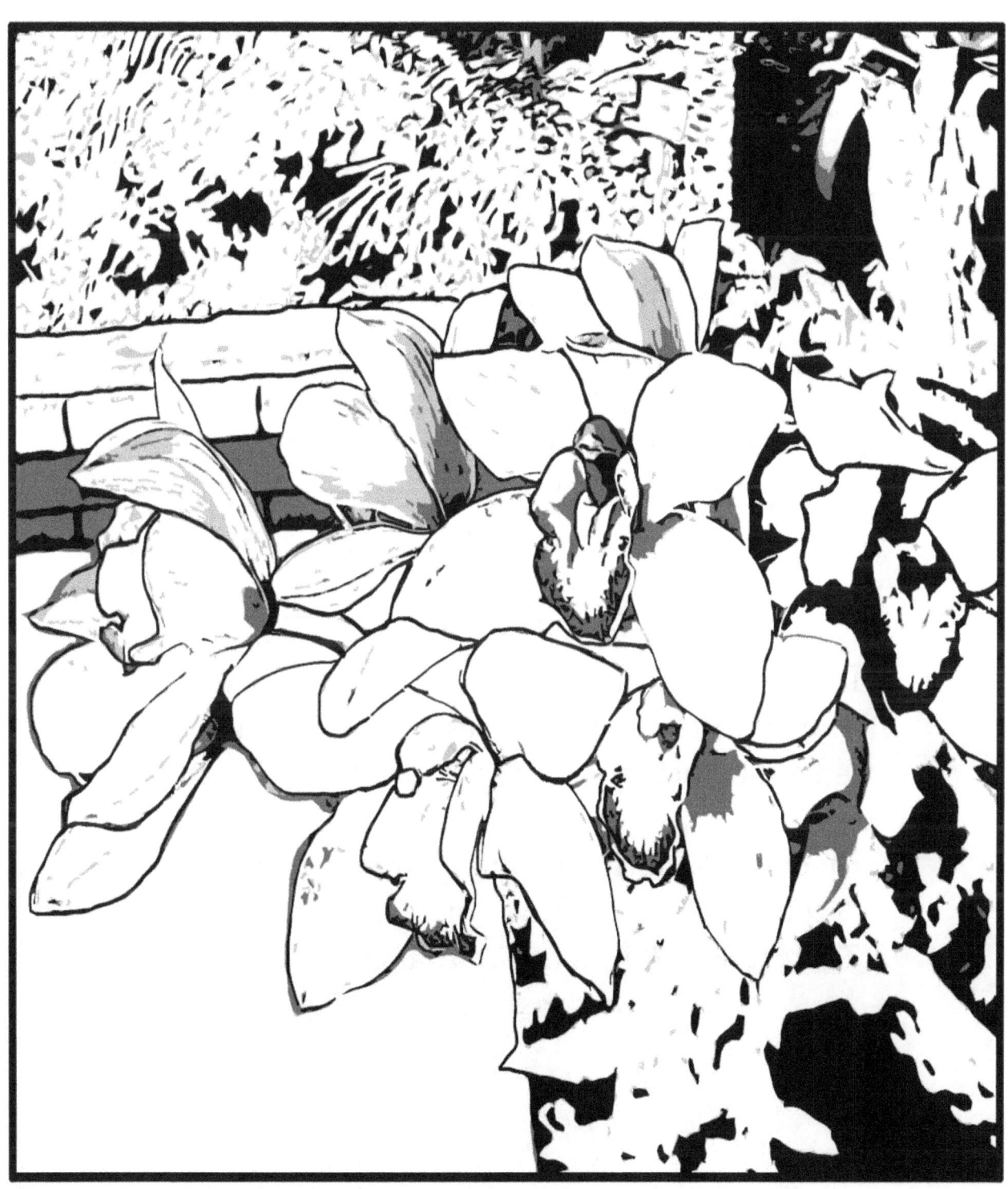

Rare flowers and plants in the Conservatory of Flowers

San Francisco Cable Cars

San Francisco is the only city in the world with
a true cable car system. The cable car lines were
established in 1873. They were created by a
gentleman by the name of Andrew Smith Hallidie.

The story is told that Andrew, while
living in San Francisco, saw a terrible accident,
one in which several horses were killed as they
tried to pull heavy wagons up the steep hills there.

He created another means of transportation to
replace the horse drawn ones---the cable car.
There were 22 lines in San Francisco originally,
but only three remain today.

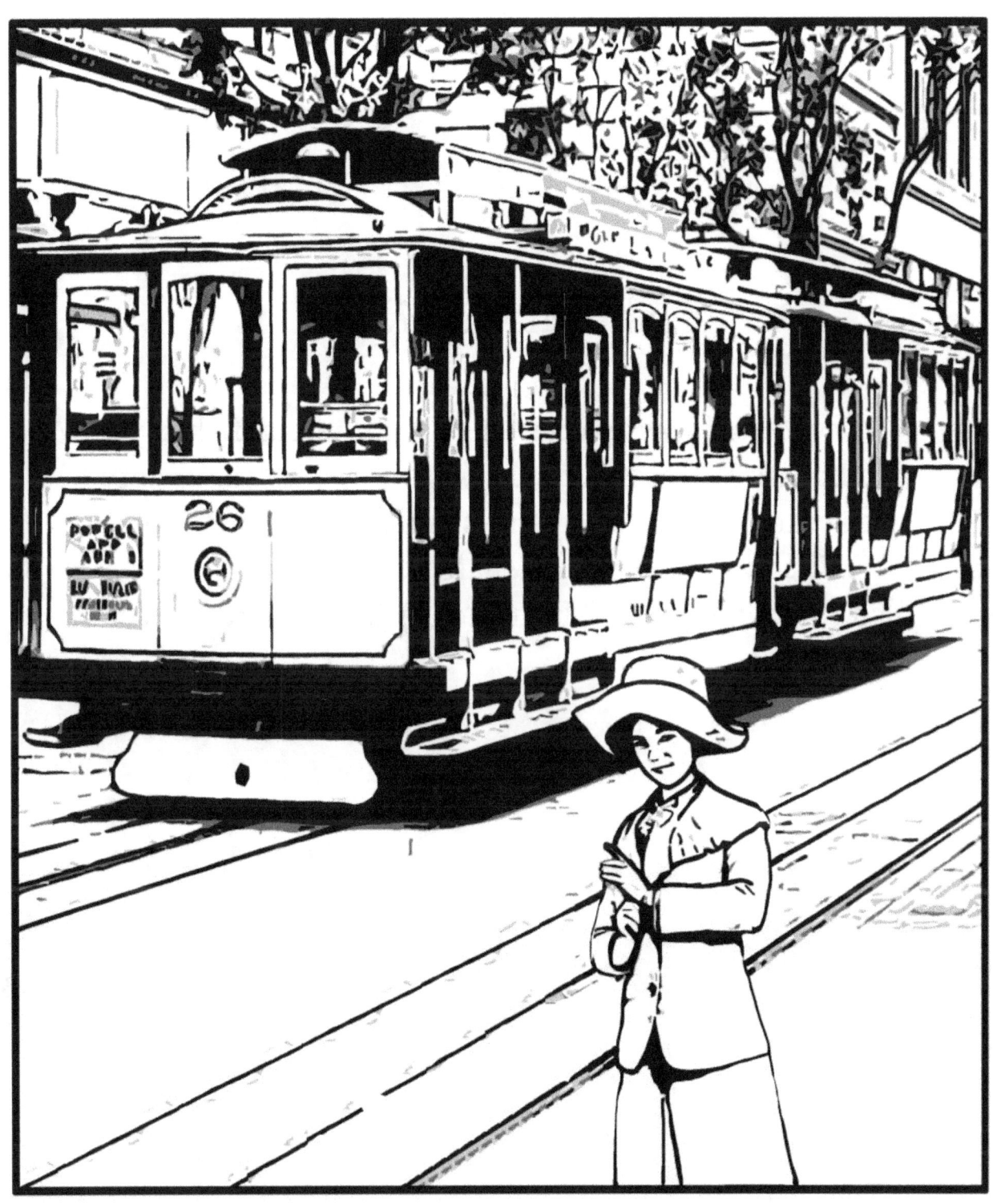

San Francisco Cable Cars - abt. 1912

Fisherman's Wharf

The Wharf was the center of commercial fishing in the late 19th century. It was known for its variety of ocean fish and Dungeness crab. The Wharf today is lined with shops and seafood restaurants. It is also the home of the Maritime National Historic Park.

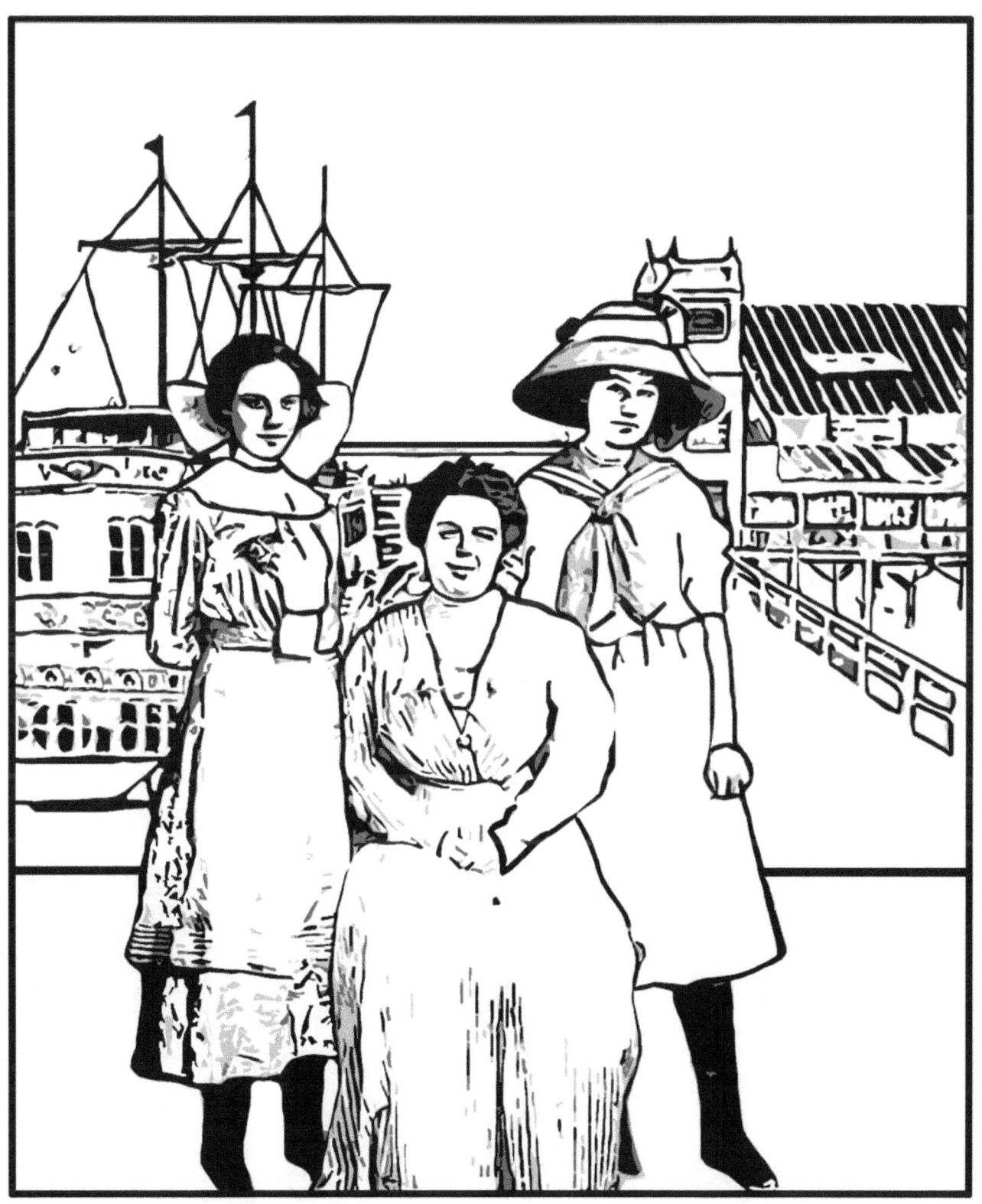

Ladies posing at the San Francisco Fisherman's Wharf - 1915

The C.A. Thayer

The C.A. Thayer is a schooner that was built in 1894. She is now at the Maritime National Historic Park at Fisherman's Wharf. She is a three-masted schooner and 219 feet long. This schooner was the ship used in the original version of the movie, "Mutiny on the Bounty."

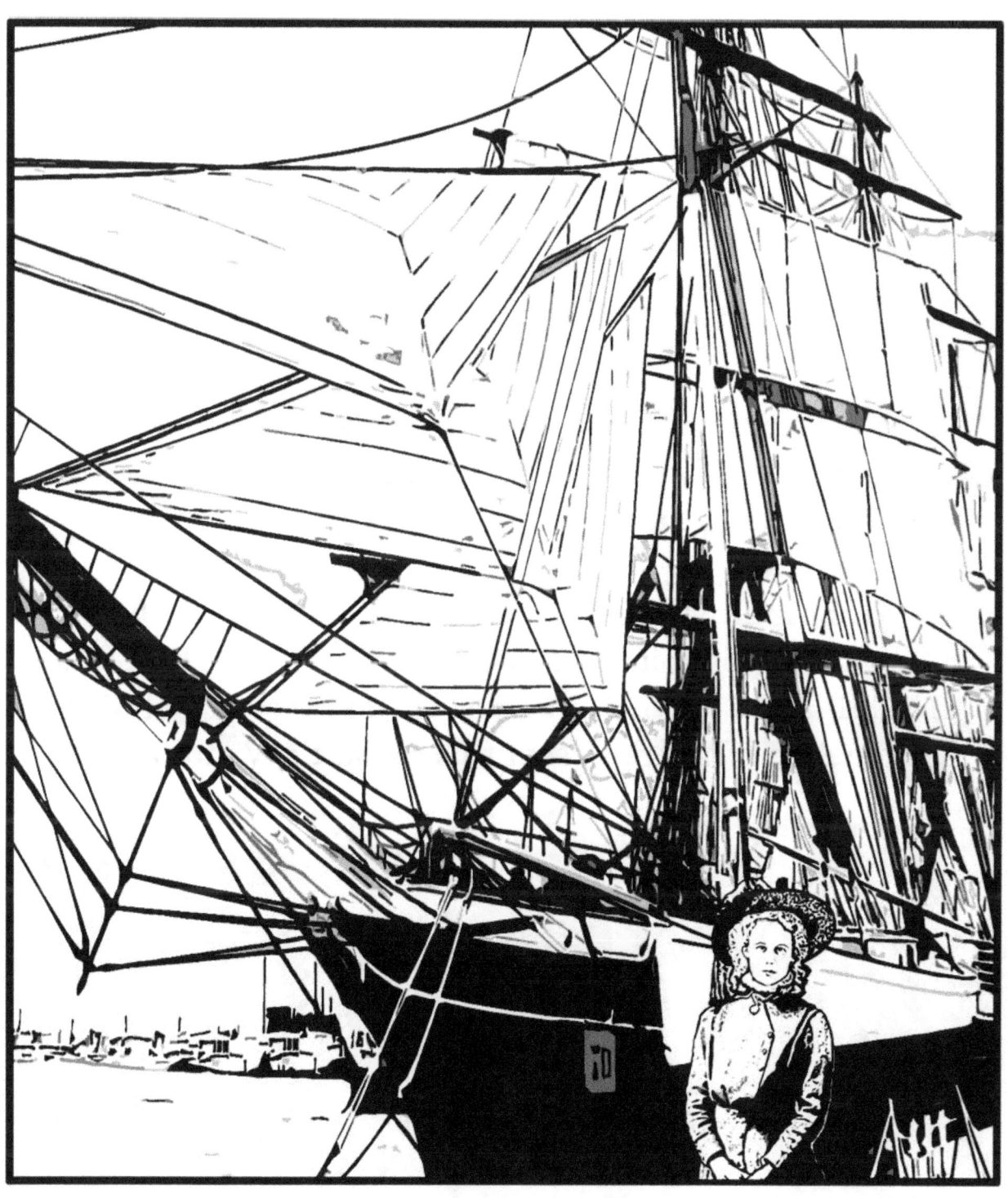

The C.A. Thayer in the Maritime National Historic Park - 1900's

The Romantic Victorian Era

Just as this portrait of a lovely young woman shows the truly romantic side of this era in San Francisco - so do many of the buildings that were erected during these years.

The beautiful Conservatory of Flowers in 1879, the romantic buildings in Golden Gate park in the early 1800's, the Cliff House in 1896, and even the many colorful homes built in Alamo Park represent this romantic, Victorian era.

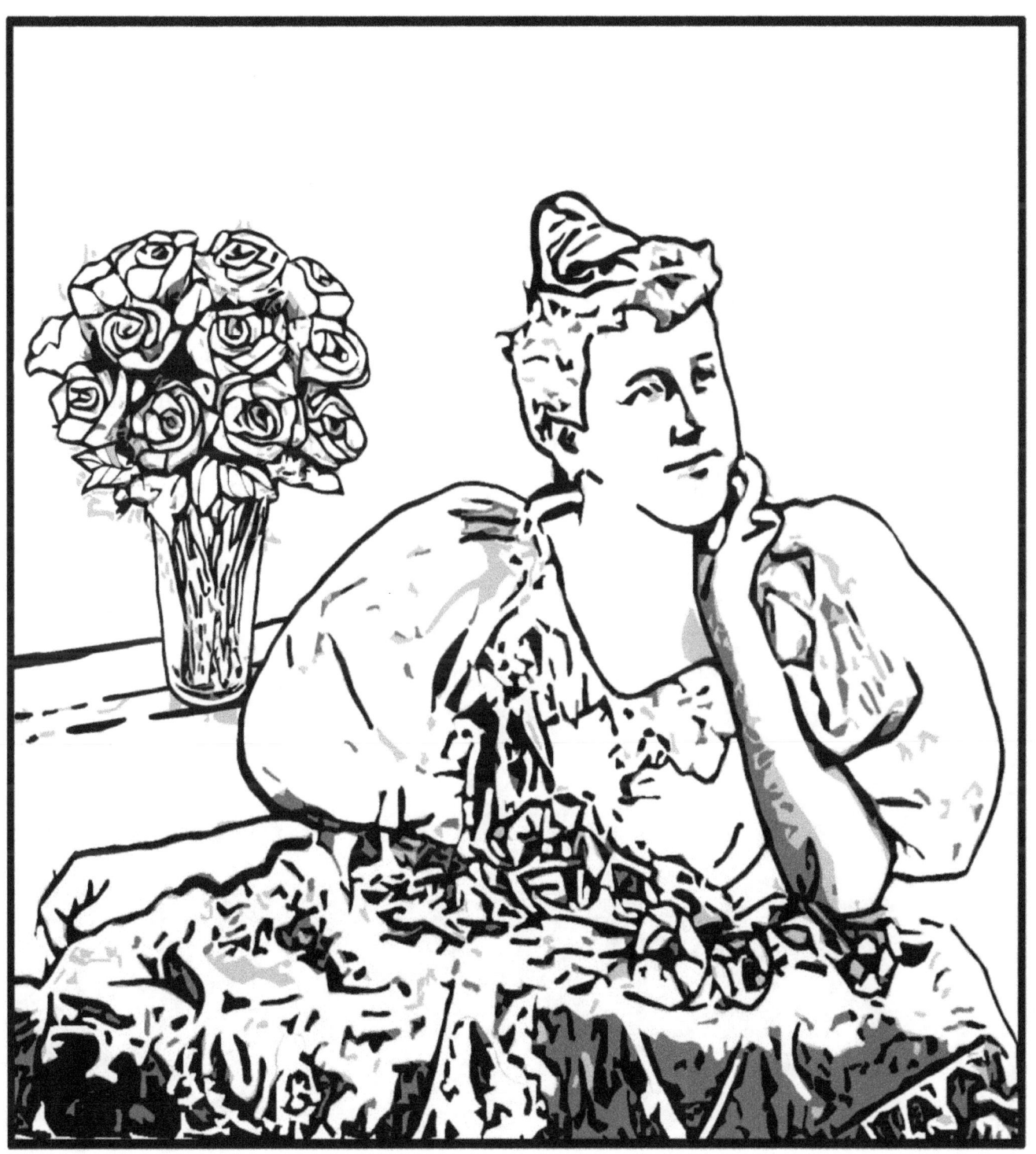

The Victorian Era - Late 1800's

Japanese Tea Gardens

The Japanese Tea Gardens were created in 1894, as a Japanese Village, for the Mid-Winter International Exposition. They were designed by Makato Hagiwara. The Drum Bridge was part of the gardens then, and remains there still today.

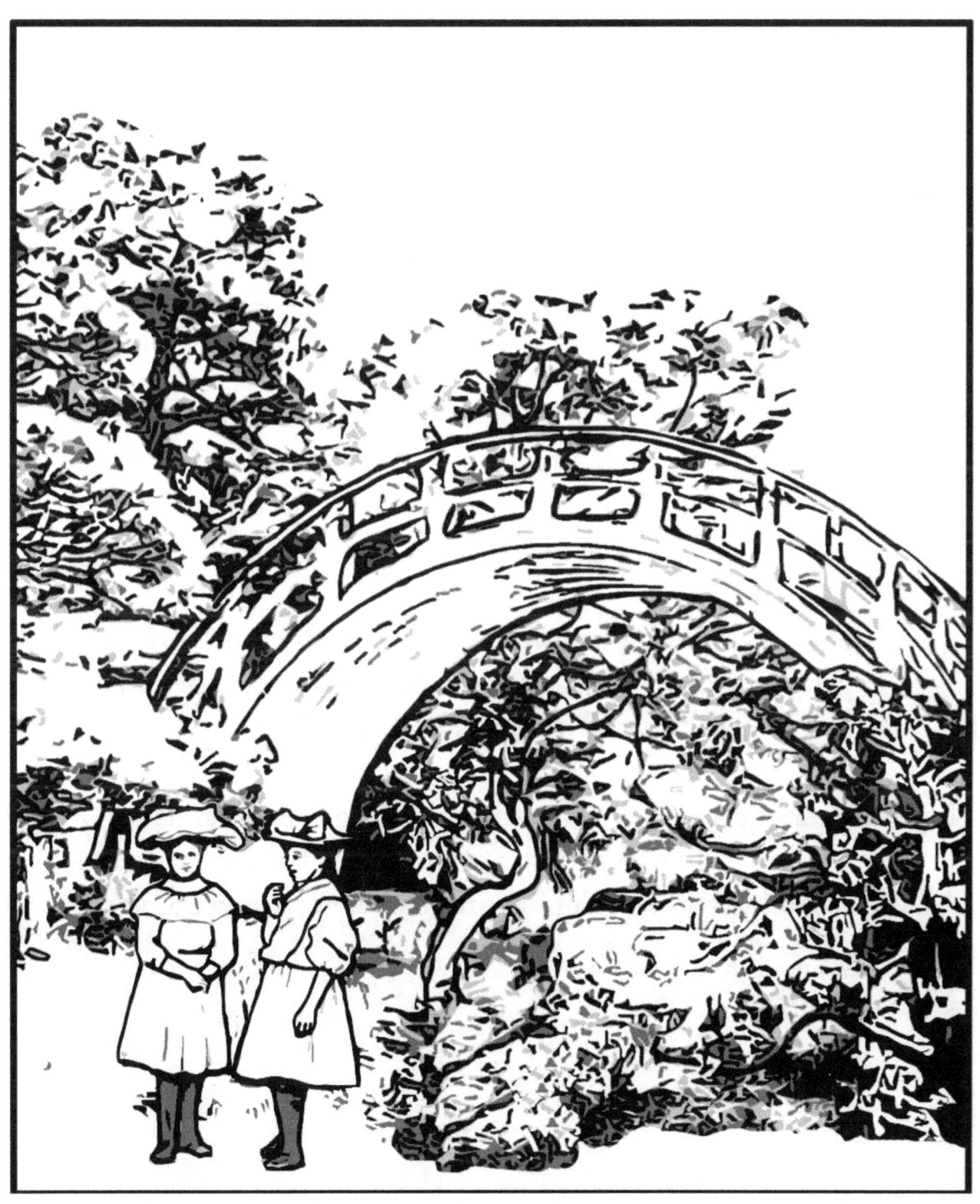

The Japanese Tea Gardens in Golden Gate Park -"The Drum Bridge" 1902

The Cliff House of San Francisco

The famous Cliff House went up in flames and burnt to the ground on September 7, 1907. The beautiful building that is pictured here, with its lovely towers and turrets, was the pride of San Francisco.

The eight story victorian building stood from 1896 to 1907. The original, earlier version was not as ornate as this one and was built in 1863.

After the 1907 fire, another building was erected--a more simpler one. A fourth version is still standing today. The food is still wonderful, and the view is spectacular.

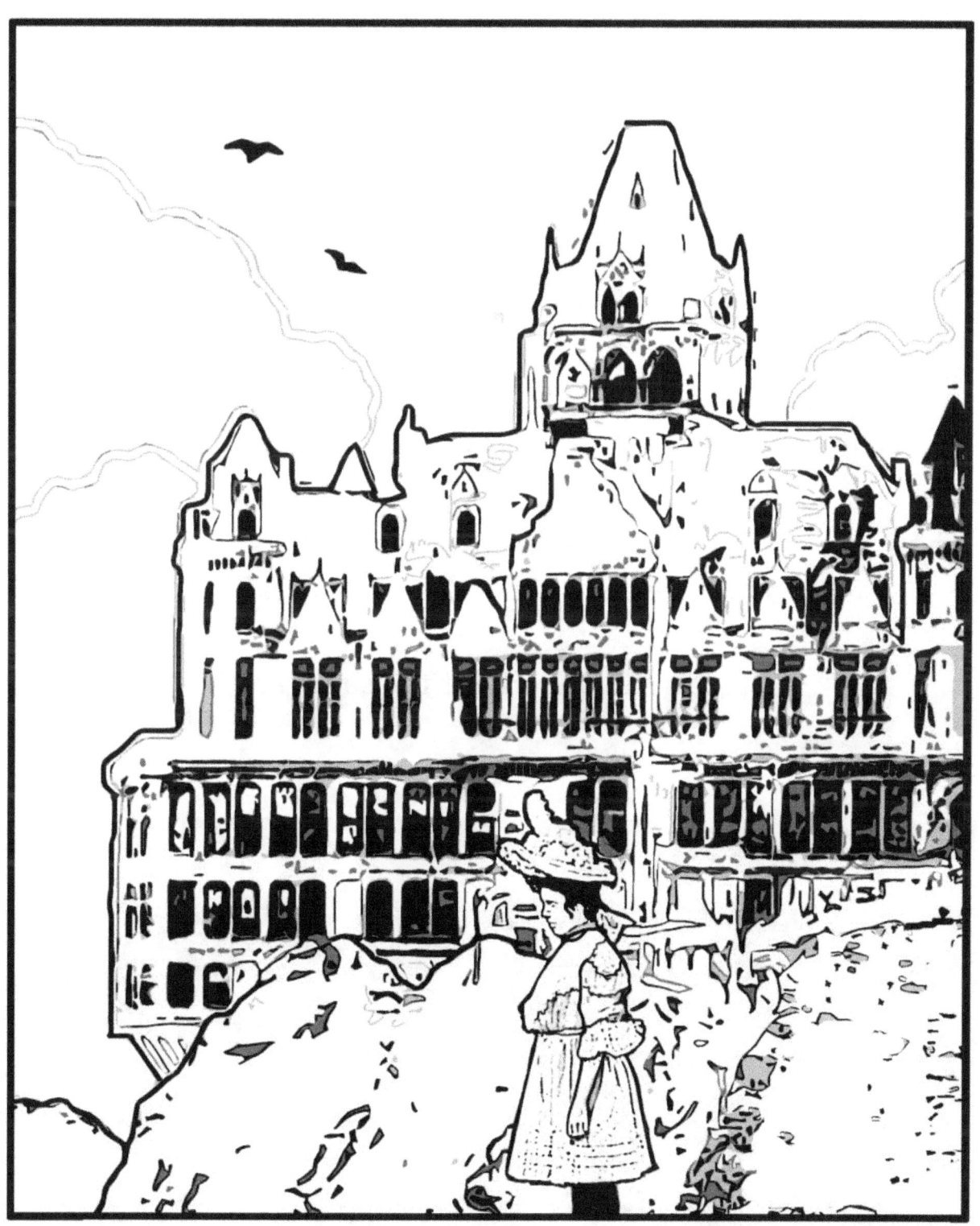

'Watching others swimming"- The San Francisco Cliff House -1900

The Golden Gate Park Band

The Golden Gate Park Band has been giving concerts in the park every sunday since 1882. The band was founded in that year and started with only twelve musicians. Today, the band is still giving concerts at the Spreckels Temple of Music, in the Music Concourse, in Golden Gate Park.

(Pictured is a band of the same era.)

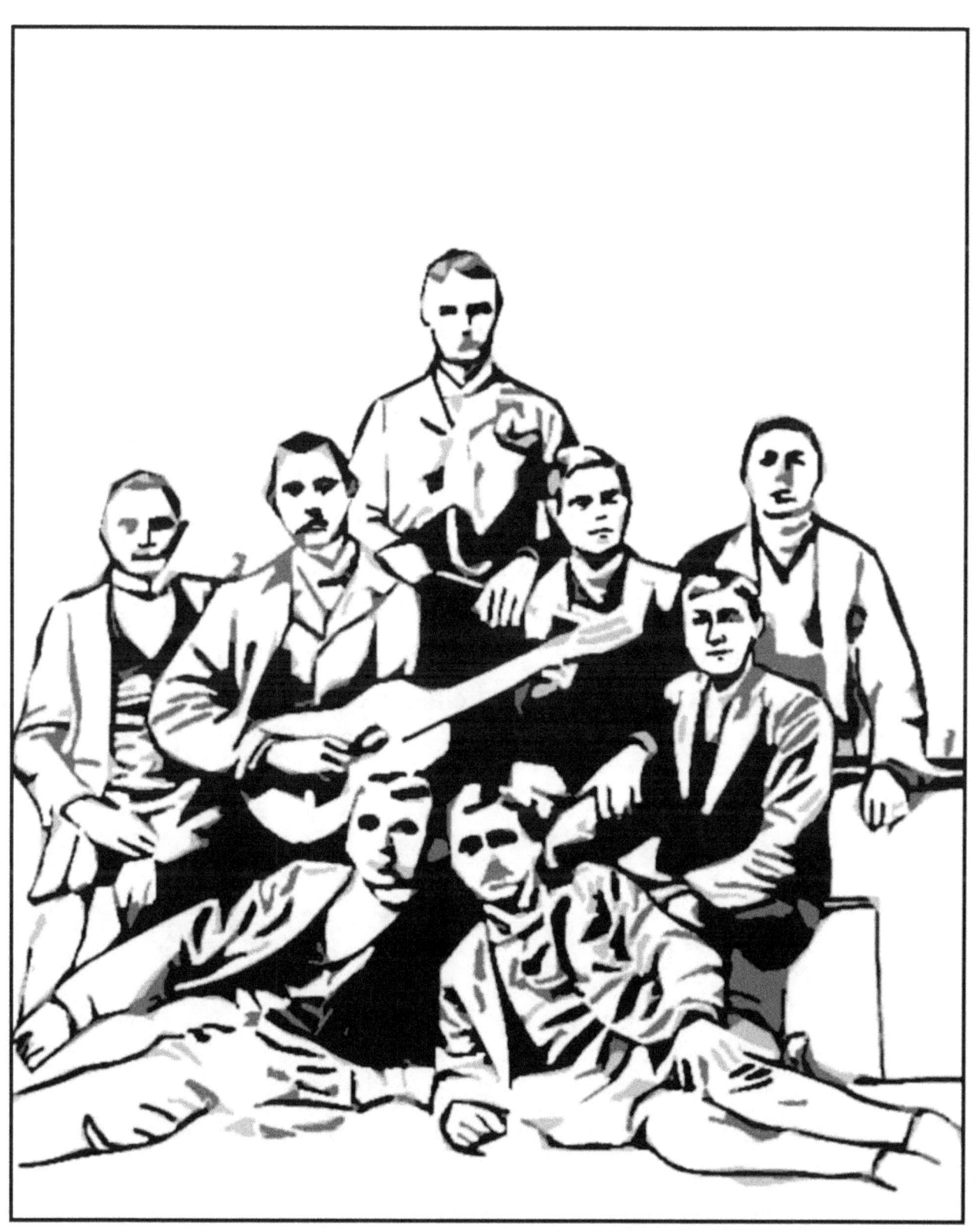

Gentlemen of a band - 1890's

The Palace of Fine Arts

The Palace of Fine Arts is one of the early landmarks in San Francisco. It was built for the Panama-Pacific International Exposition in 1915. It was to house the art on display during the Exposition, and was one of the few buildings to remain afterwards. It is also still in its original setting. Although the building has been renovated several times, it still maintains its original design and classic character.

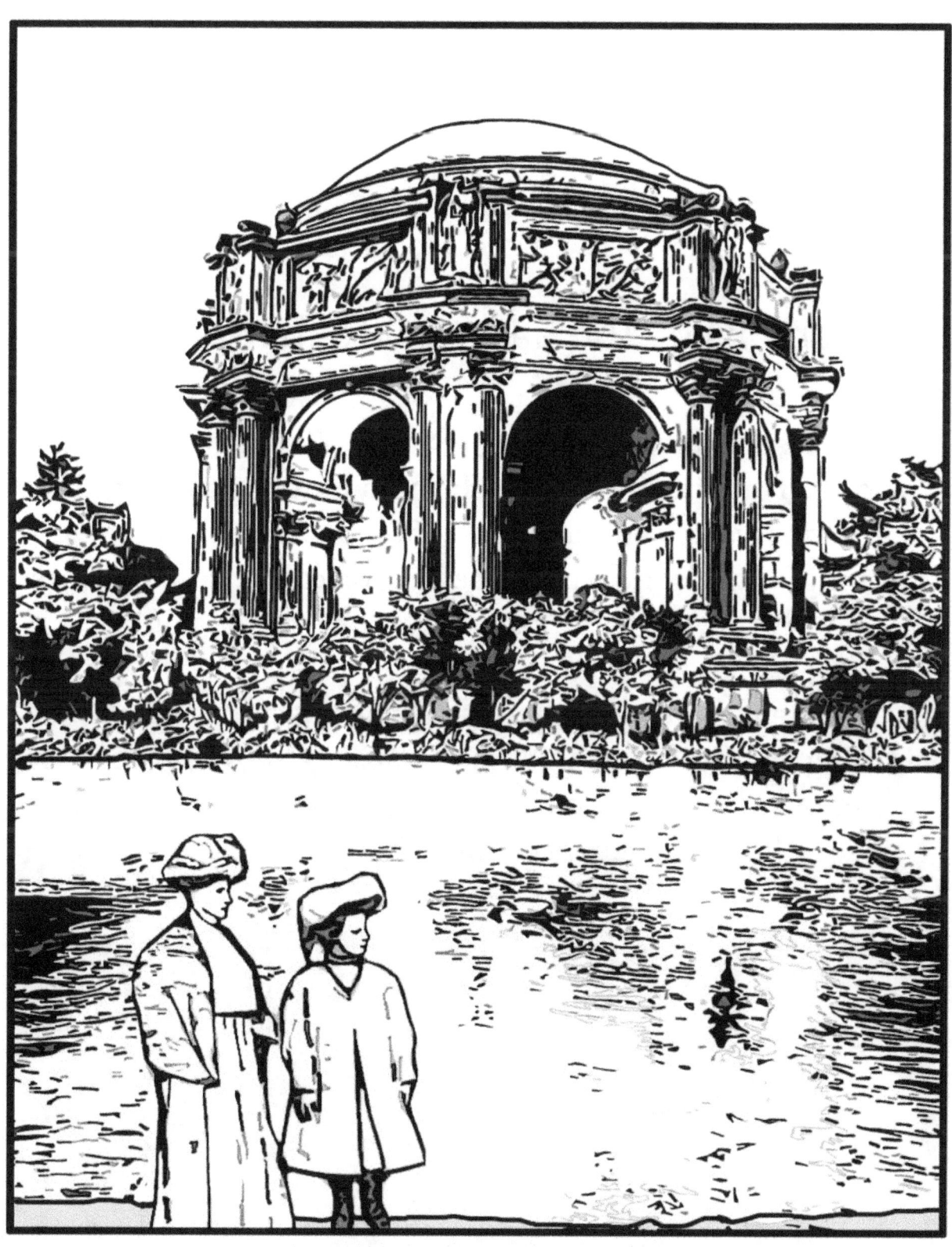

The Palace of Fine Arts - 1915

Fashions of The Late 1800's Early 1900's

The Industrial revolution of the late 1800's and early 1900's made a great difference in the fashion industry. The sewing machine was invented in the 1850's in Europe; and then clothing, with the help of the sewing machine, became more affordable and more readily available to the public.

Department stores sprang up in all the big cities and offered clothing on display and in different sizes. The Victorian style fashions were still popular, but sleeves and dress lengths were becoming shorter.

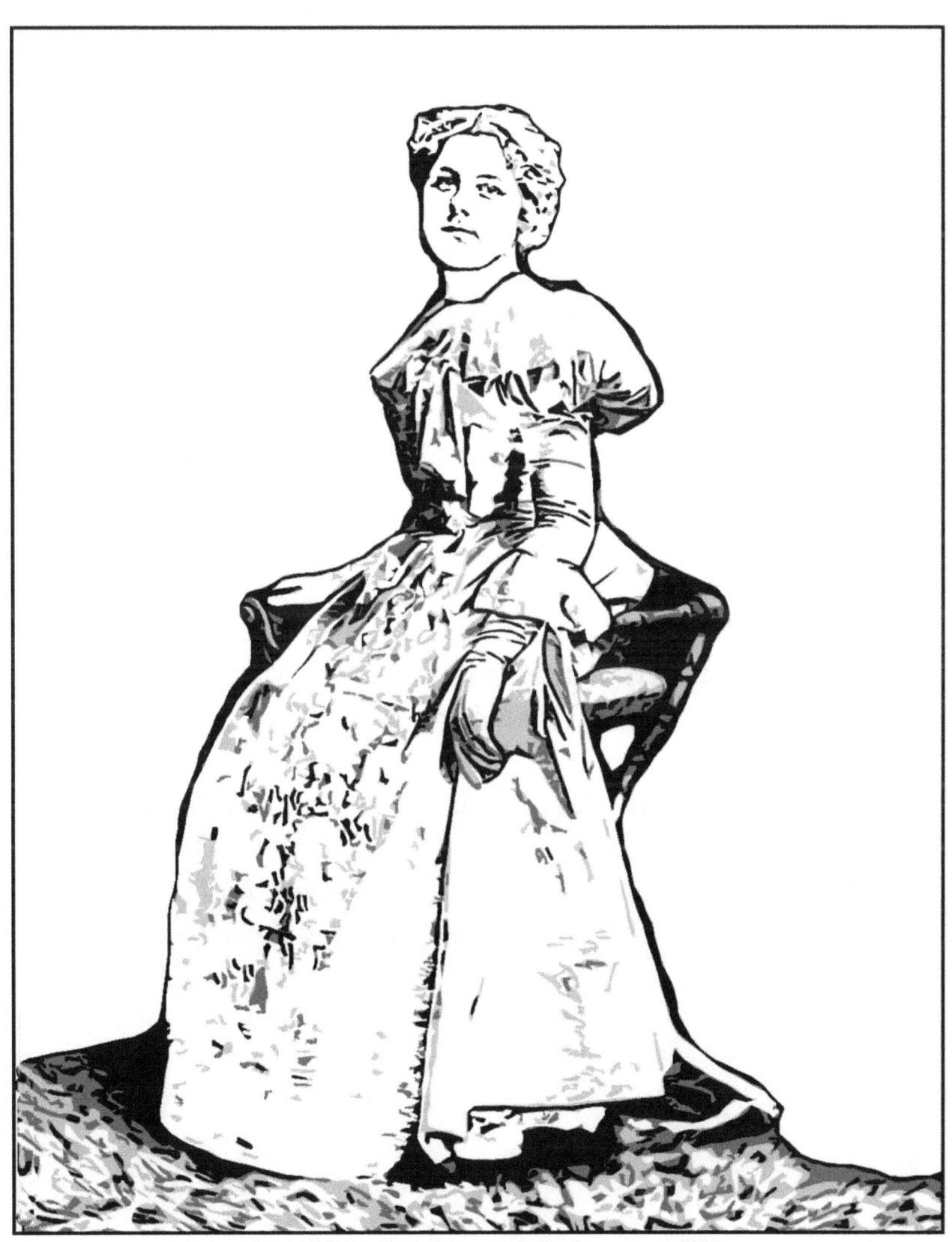

Dressed for the Costume Ball - abt. 1890

Alcatraz Island

Alcatraz Island is a 22 acre island. A lighthouse was built there in 1854. It was replaced by a tower in 1909, which is still there. In 1907 it became a prison for the military.

In the 1920's and 30's it became a prison for some of the most notorious criminals, such as Al Capone, Billy Kelly "Machine Gun Kelly", and the famous Bird Man of Alcatraz, Robert Stroud.

It was given to the US government in 1933 and became a federal prison until 1963. It was known as the prison that no man could escape from. Only three men ever got off the Island, and were believed to drown in the bay--they were never found.

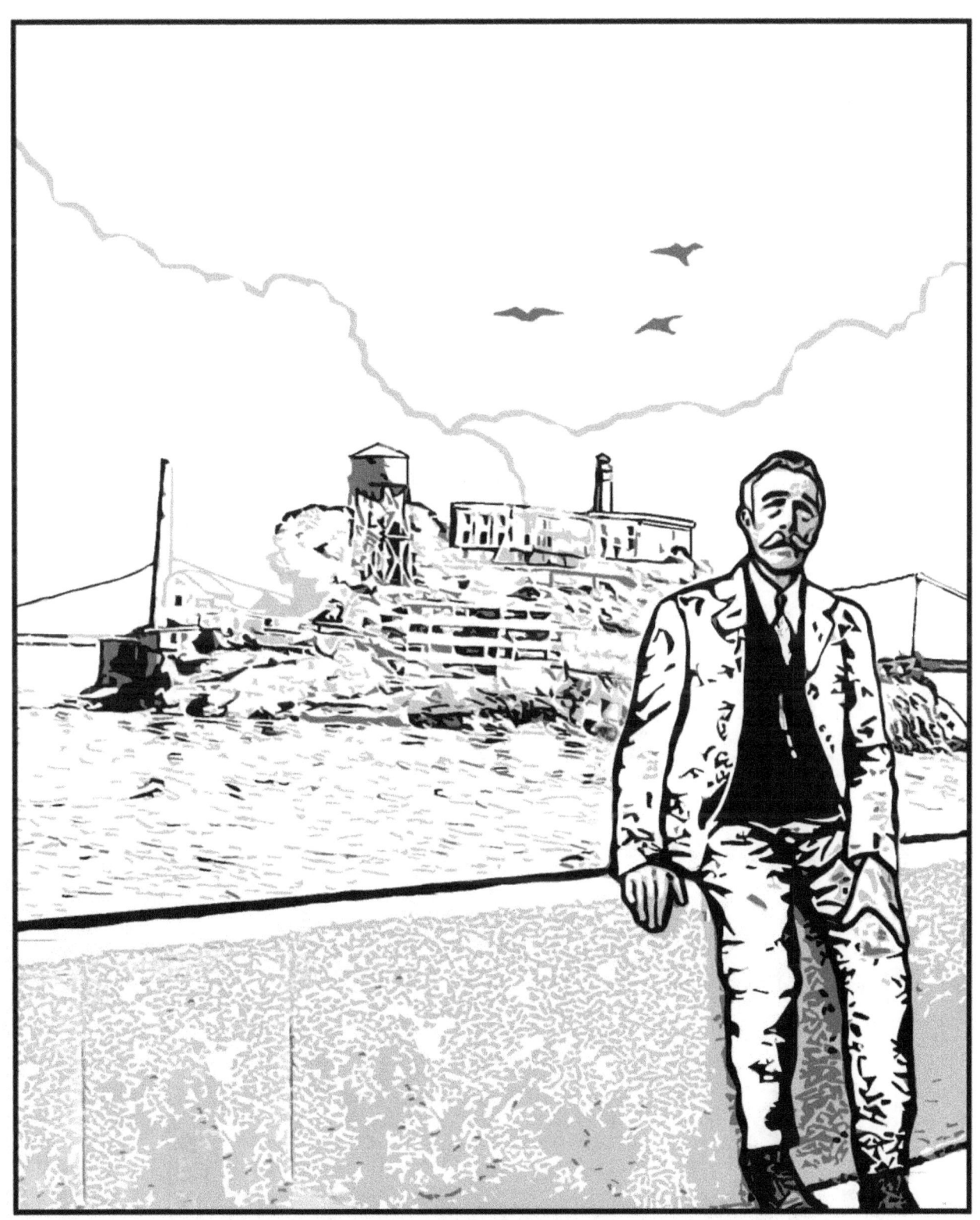

Alcatraz Island, known as the "Rock" - 1920

Early Photography

This is an early photograph taken in a studio in San Francisco. The first photo process was called the Daguerreotype. It was very expensive, and could only produce one photo at a time. Those having their pictures taken had to remain still for several minutes, as the exposure time was almost 15 minutes long.

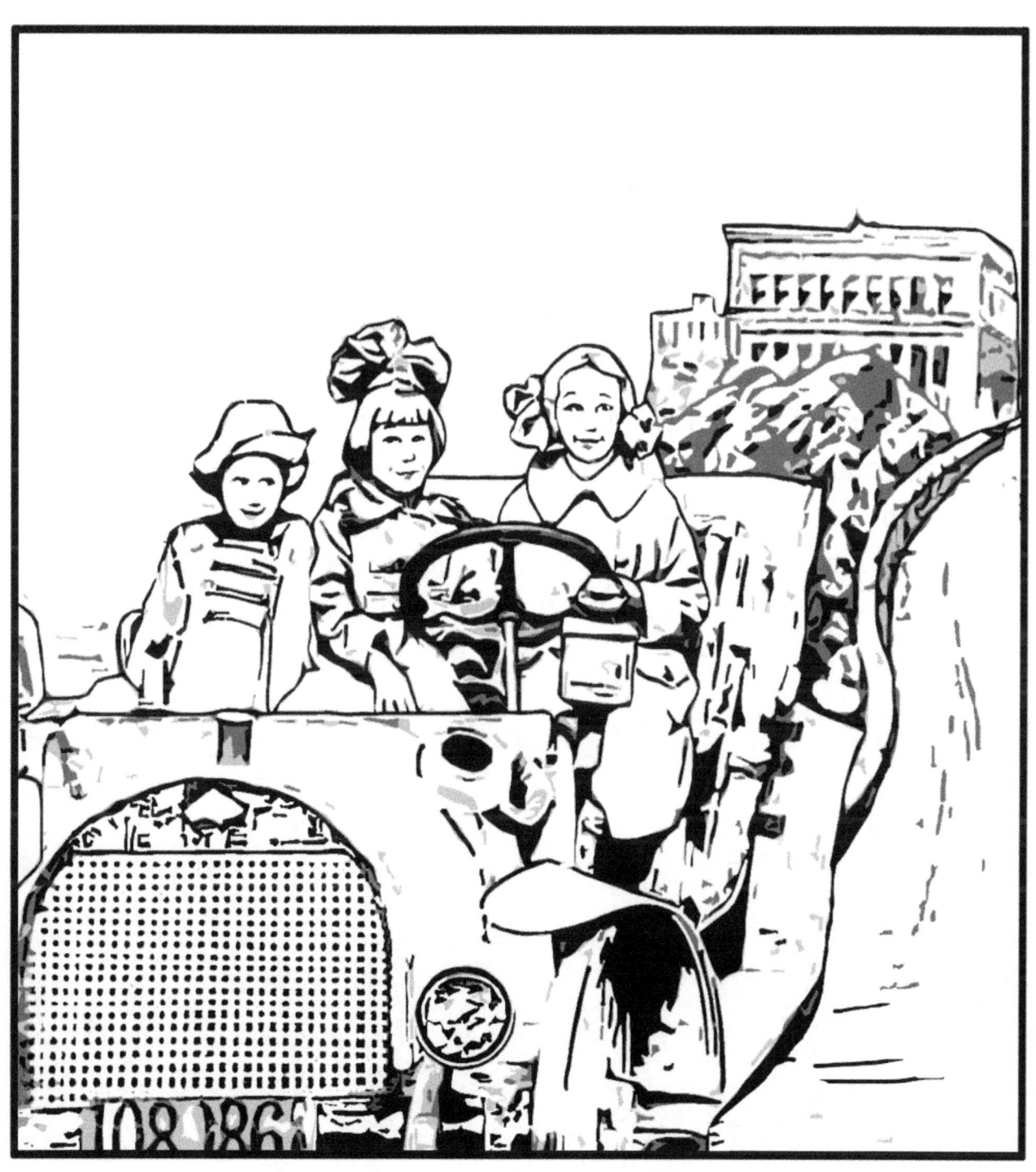

A San Francisco photography studio - 1923

Child's Portrait

In the 1920's, photographers actually used a fake bird (some made of brass) to get children's attention while taking their photo. Some birdies could even make a whistling sound when a bulb connected to it was squeezed. This is where we get the classic phrase, "watch the birdie" while taking a photo.

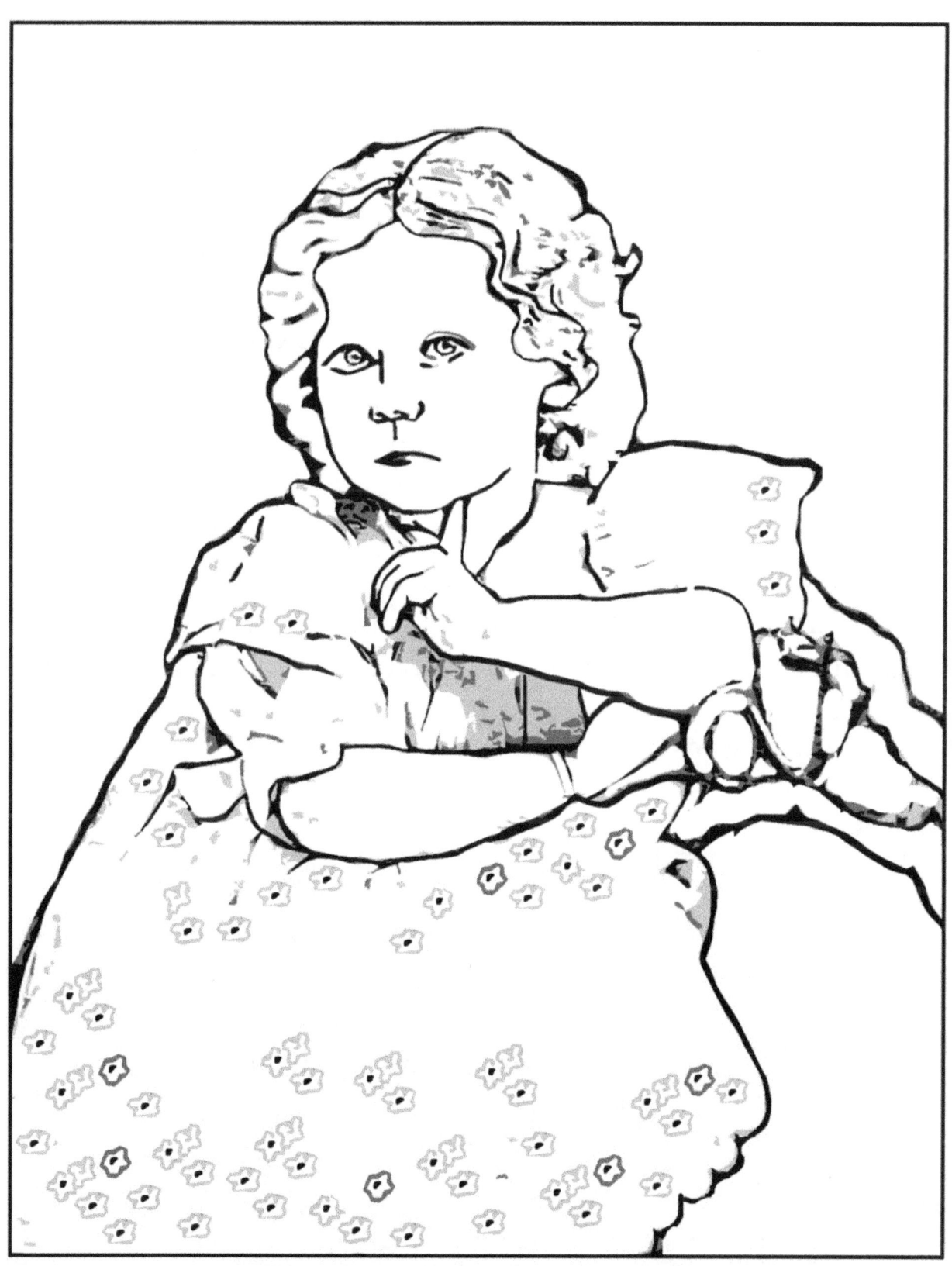

Portrait of a young girl - abt. 1900

San Francisco's China Town

China Town was started in the mid-nineteenth century. Most of the Chinese at the time had jobs with the Central Pacific Railroad. In 1906, most of the town was destroyed by fire caused by the great earthquake. In the 1920's , the new buildings were more decorative. Chinese New Year dates back to the 1860's. The parade dragon represents good luck.

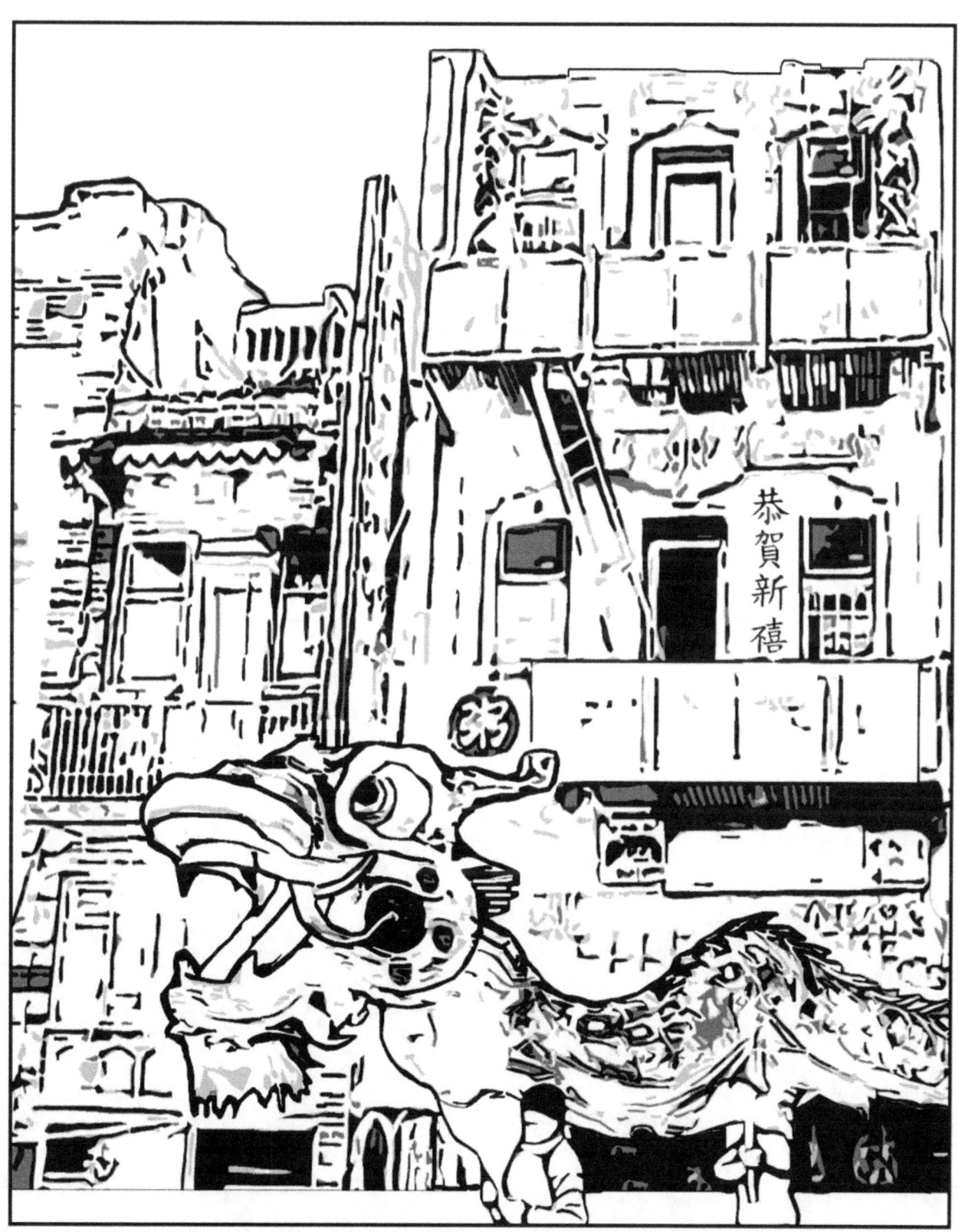

San Francisco's China Town - Chinese New Year

The Palace of The Legion of Honor

The Palace of The Legion of Honor was completed in 1924. It was dedicated to the men of California who died in battle during World War I in France. It was a smaller replica of the 18th century original, in Paris, France. The building was donated to the city of San Francisco by the Spreckels family.

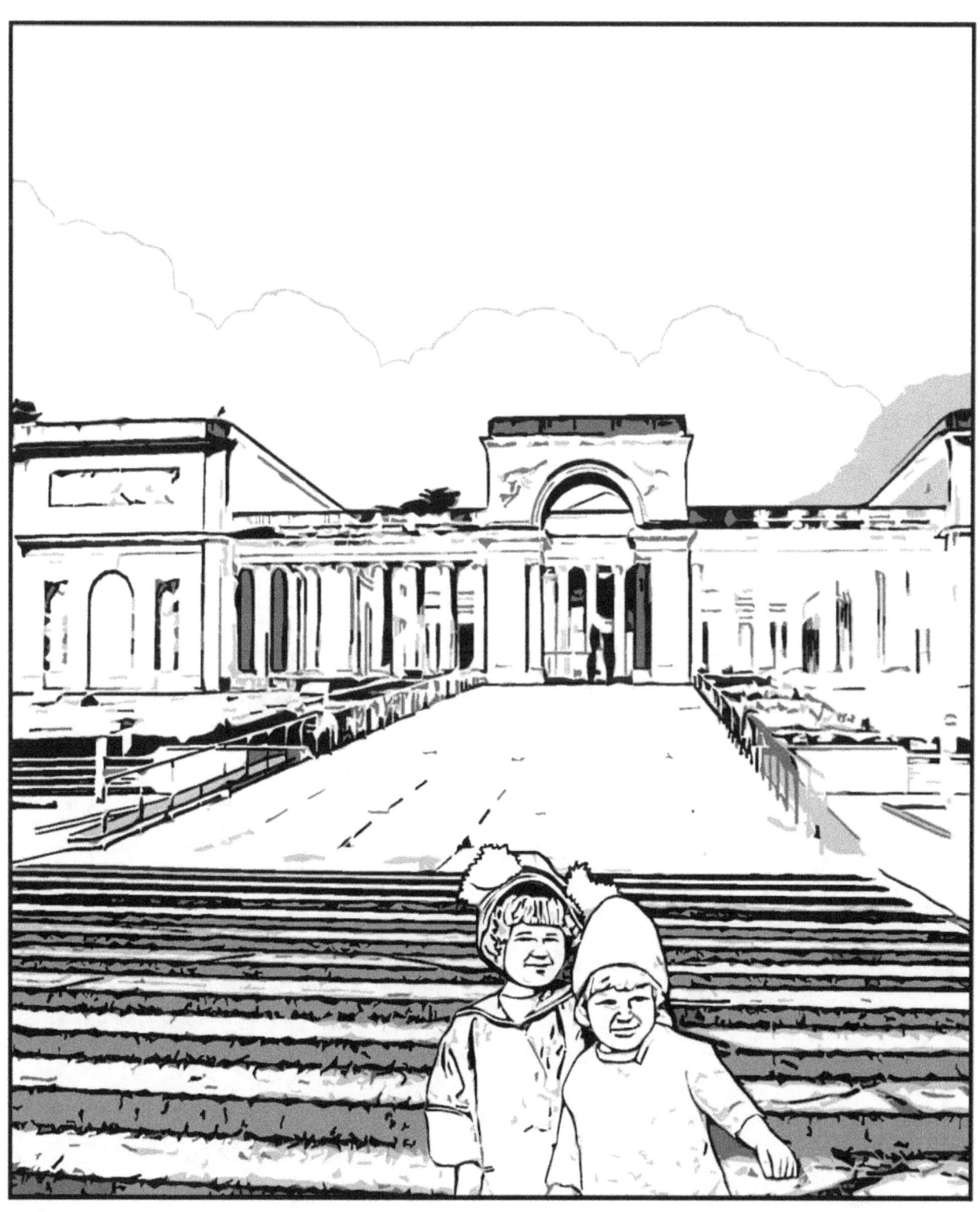

The Palace of The Legion of Honor - 1924

The Collection of Art at The Legion of Honor

The art collection in the Legion of Honor in San Francisco is mainly composed of European art. The beautiful replica of "The Thinker" stands in the main courtyard of the museum.

There are works of art by famous artists, such as El Greco, Rubens, and Rembrandt, to name a few; and paintings from the Impressionist era by Monet, Cezanne, Renoir, and Degas. It is truly a magnificent museum.

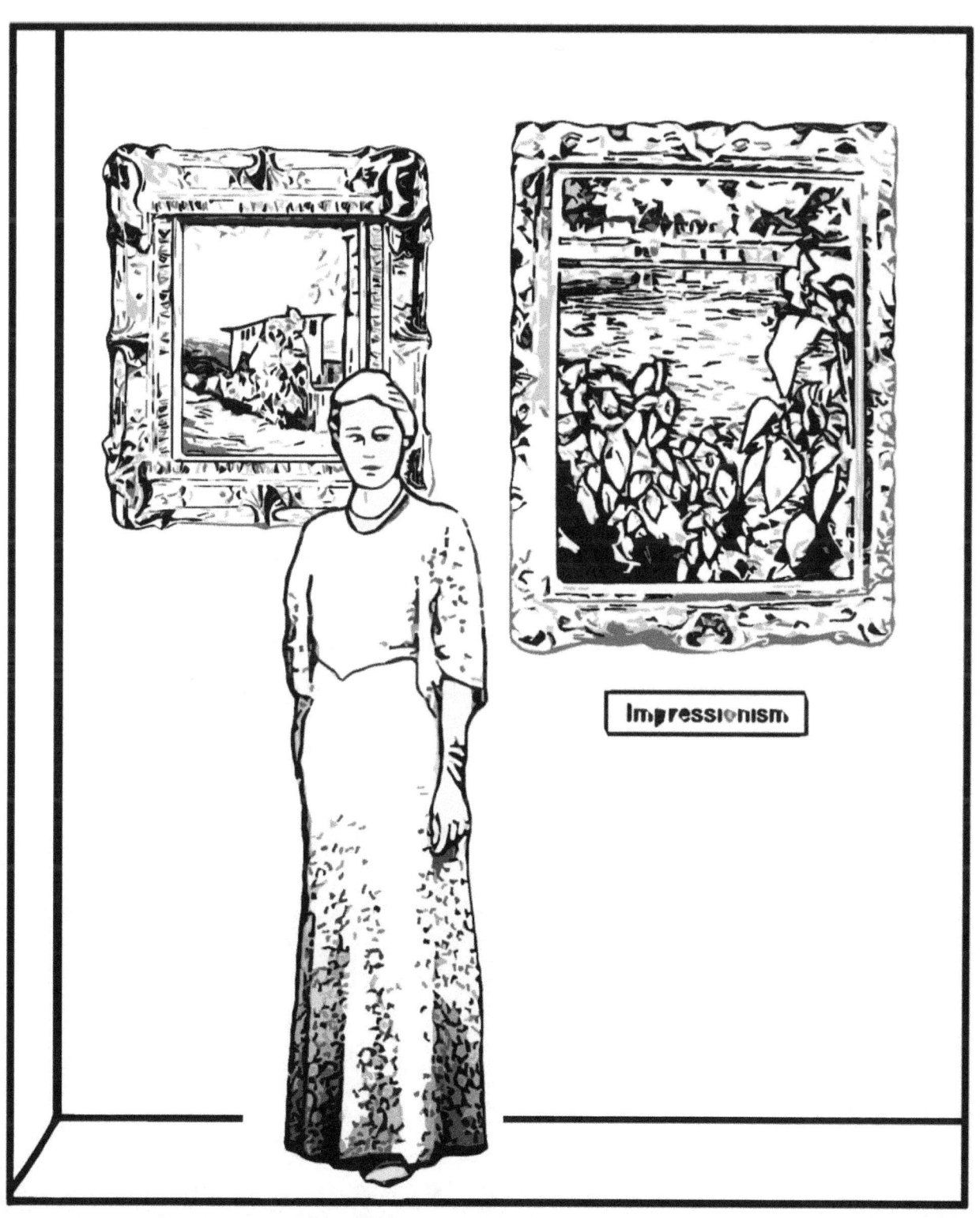

Paintings at the Palace of The Legion of Honor - 1932

A Soldier of World War I

The United States entered World War I in 1917. It was a difficult time for the soldiers in the Army, for there were few supplies and little aircraft. In spite of all the obstacles, however, and because of brave men and valiant leaders, battles were successfully won against the German Army. The courage and competency of the American troops were proven and an Armistice was declared in November 1918.

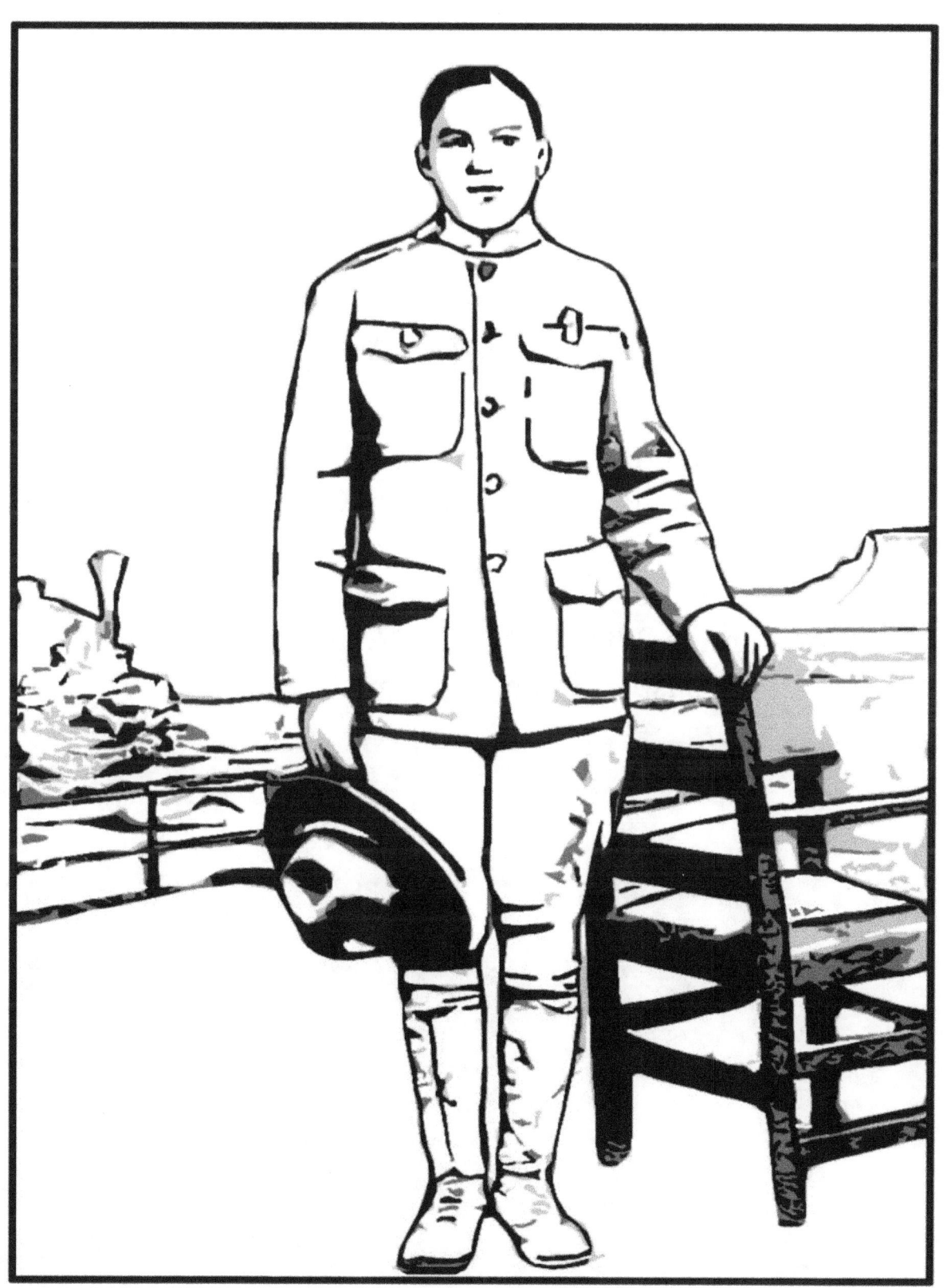

A Soldier from World War I - 1917

Golden Gate Bridge

They started building the Golden Gate Bridge in 1933. It was built to connect San Francisco to Marin County. It took 4 years to finish the bridge at the cost of 35 million dollars, which was a great deal of money at the time. The bridge was open to the public on the 27th of May, 1937. It was the largest suspension bridge until 1964.

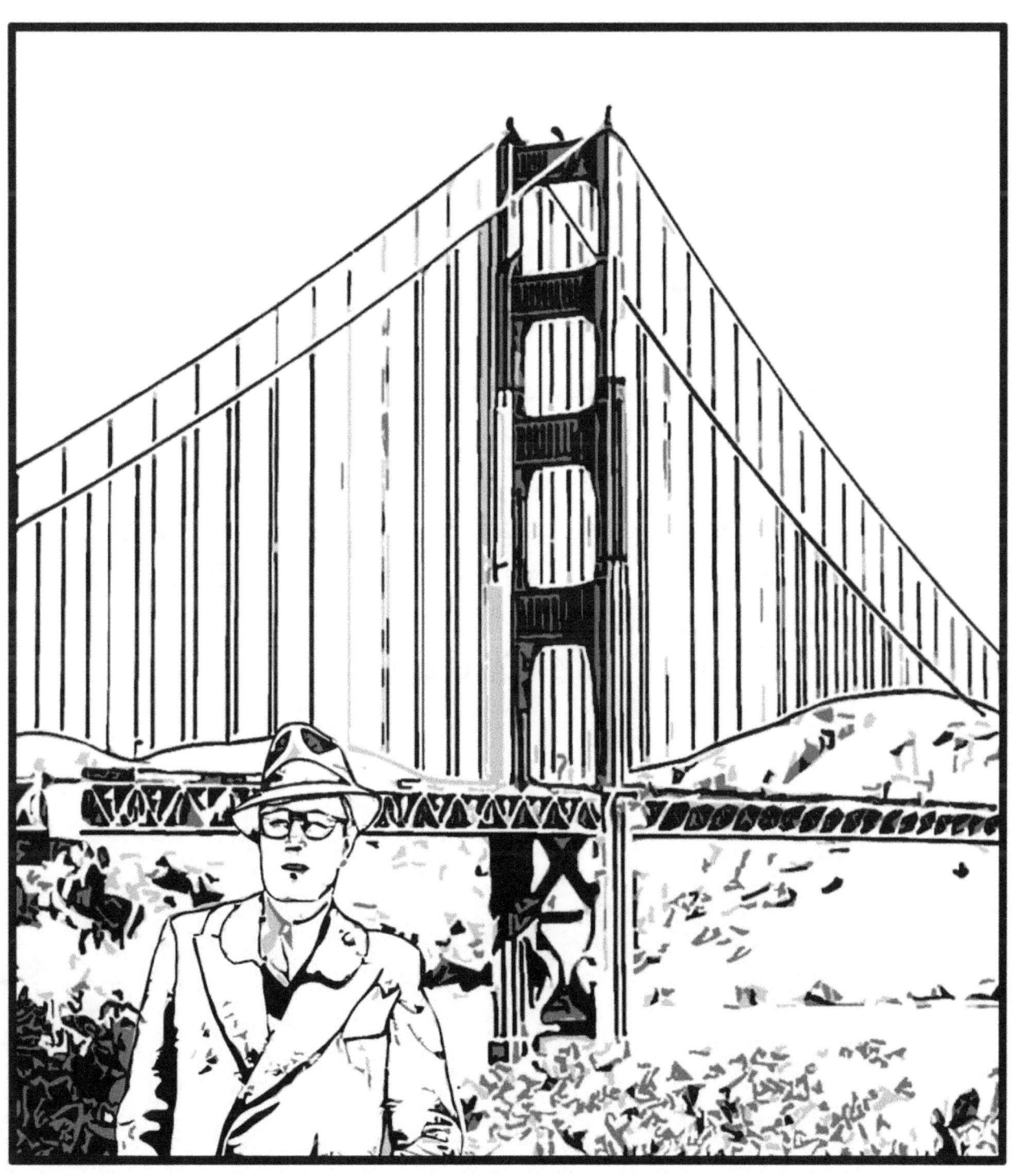

San Francisco's Golden Gate Bridge - 1937

Christmas in Early San Francisco

Christmas on Market Street in San Francisco was a magical time. Shop windows were adorned with lights and fanciful displays. The "City of Paris" department store was one of the loveliest stores of all. It was started in 1872 and remained in business for more than 100 years. The huge Christmas tree that graced its halls was over 50 feet high with over 2,000 lights and 4,000 ornaments.

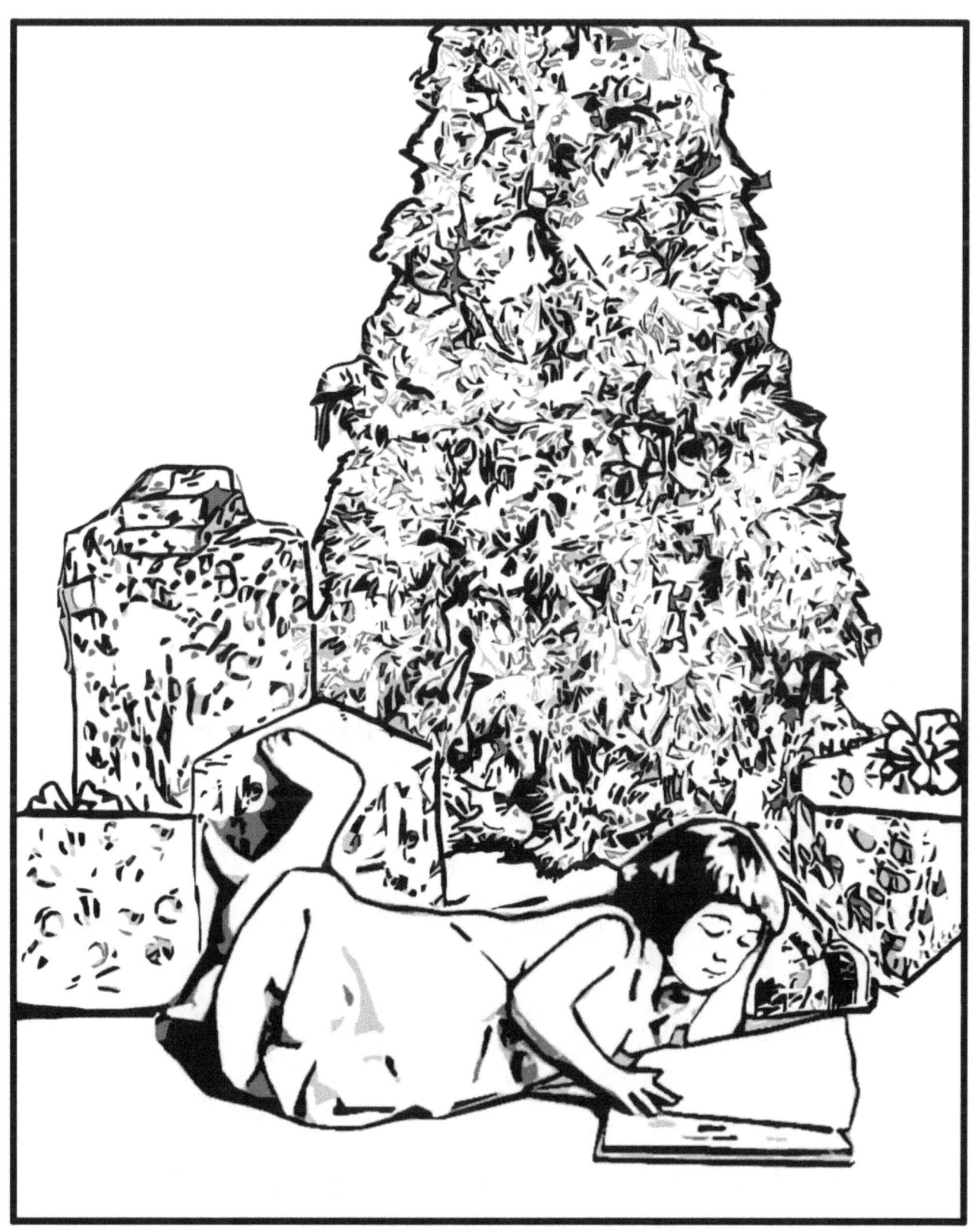

"Waiting for Christmas" - 1899

California Coastal Cities - Laguna Beach 1918

Laguna Beach only had about 300 residents in 1910. A few years later, many Impressionist artists (some from Europe) were drawn to this lovely picturesque town with its canyons, tide pools, and long beaches.

In 1918, the city of Laguna donated a building to the town's artists. Their first art show took place on July 27, 1918, and over 2,000 people attended. Laguna Beach became one of the art hubs of the Pacific Coast.

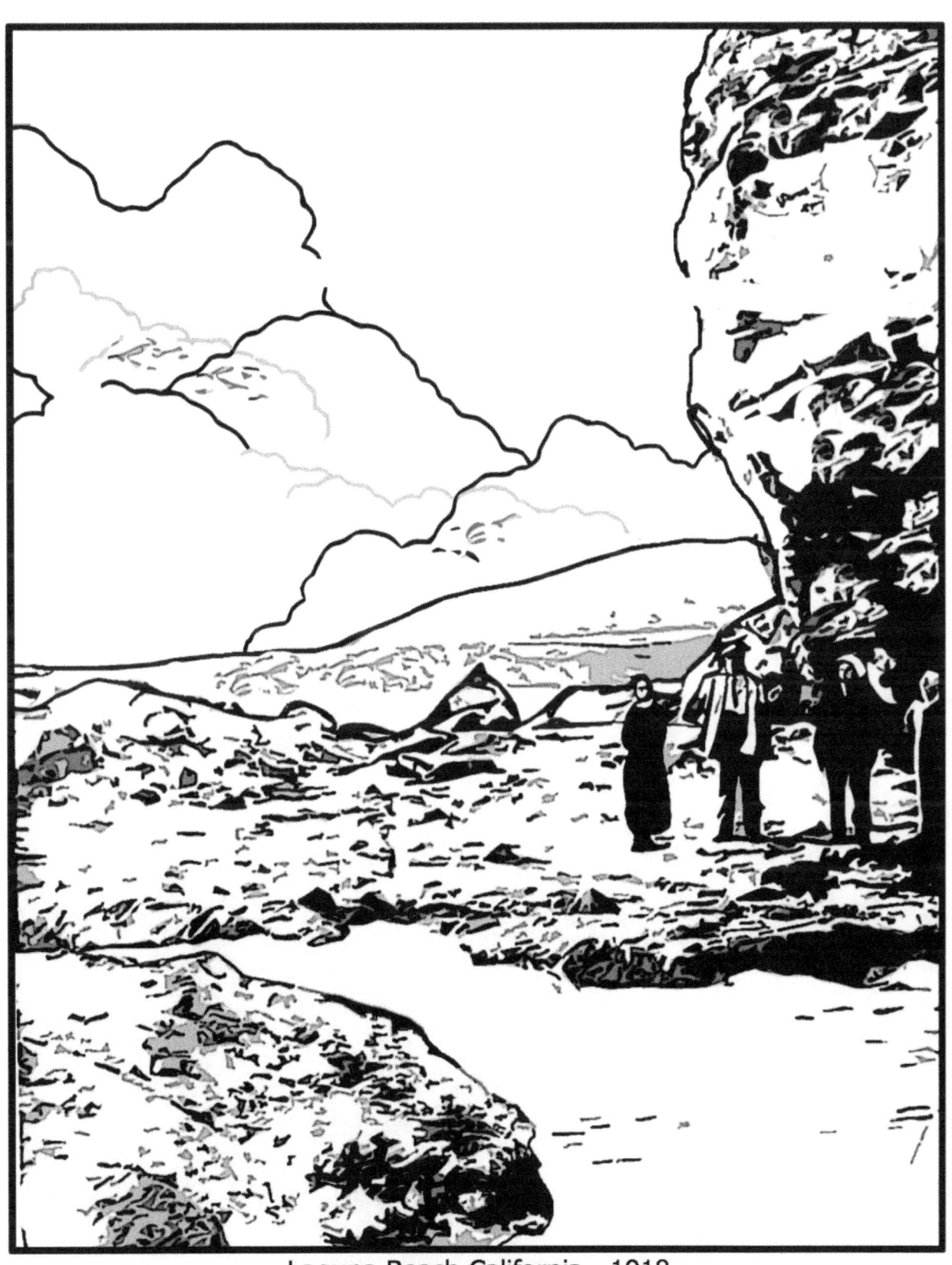

Laguna Beach, California - 1918

The Sea Side Boardwalk - Santa Cruz, California

Santa Cruz, California is home to one of the last and oldest Sea Side Boardwalks in the United States. It is 102 years old. Its "Loof Carousel" was established in 1911 and the old wooden roller coaster, "The Giant Dipper" in 1924.

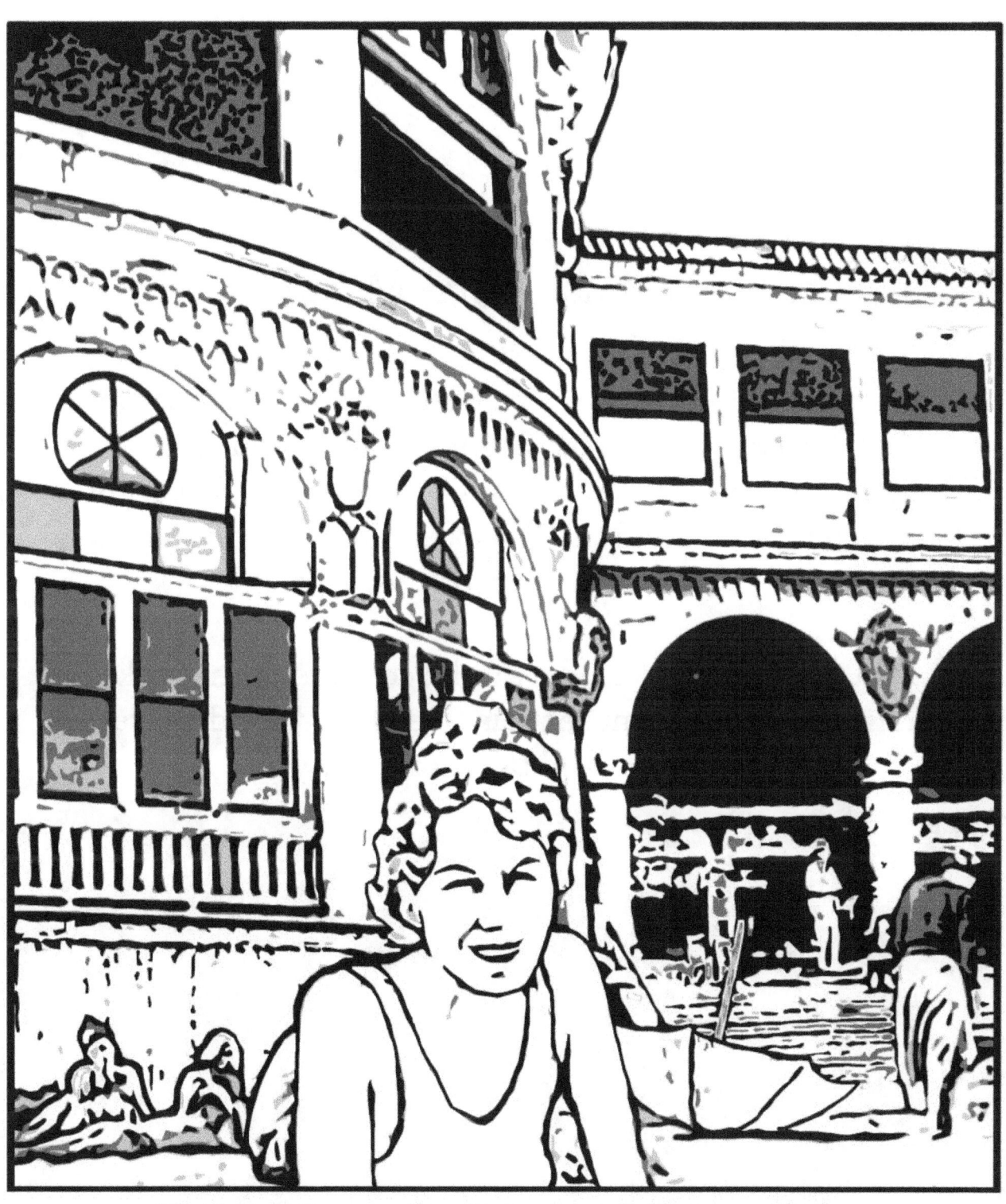

The Beach Boardwalk - Santa Cruz, California - 1920's

Yosemite National Park - Mariposa Grove

Yosemite National Park is one of the first wilderness parks in our country. In 1864, President Lincoln, in order to preserve this beautiful wilderness, signed a bill that granted Yosemite Valley and the Mariposa Grove to the state of California as a protected park.

In 1890, John Muir helped with the creation of the park. The Grizzly Giant is a giant sequoia tree. It is the oldest tree in the grove, and the second largest.

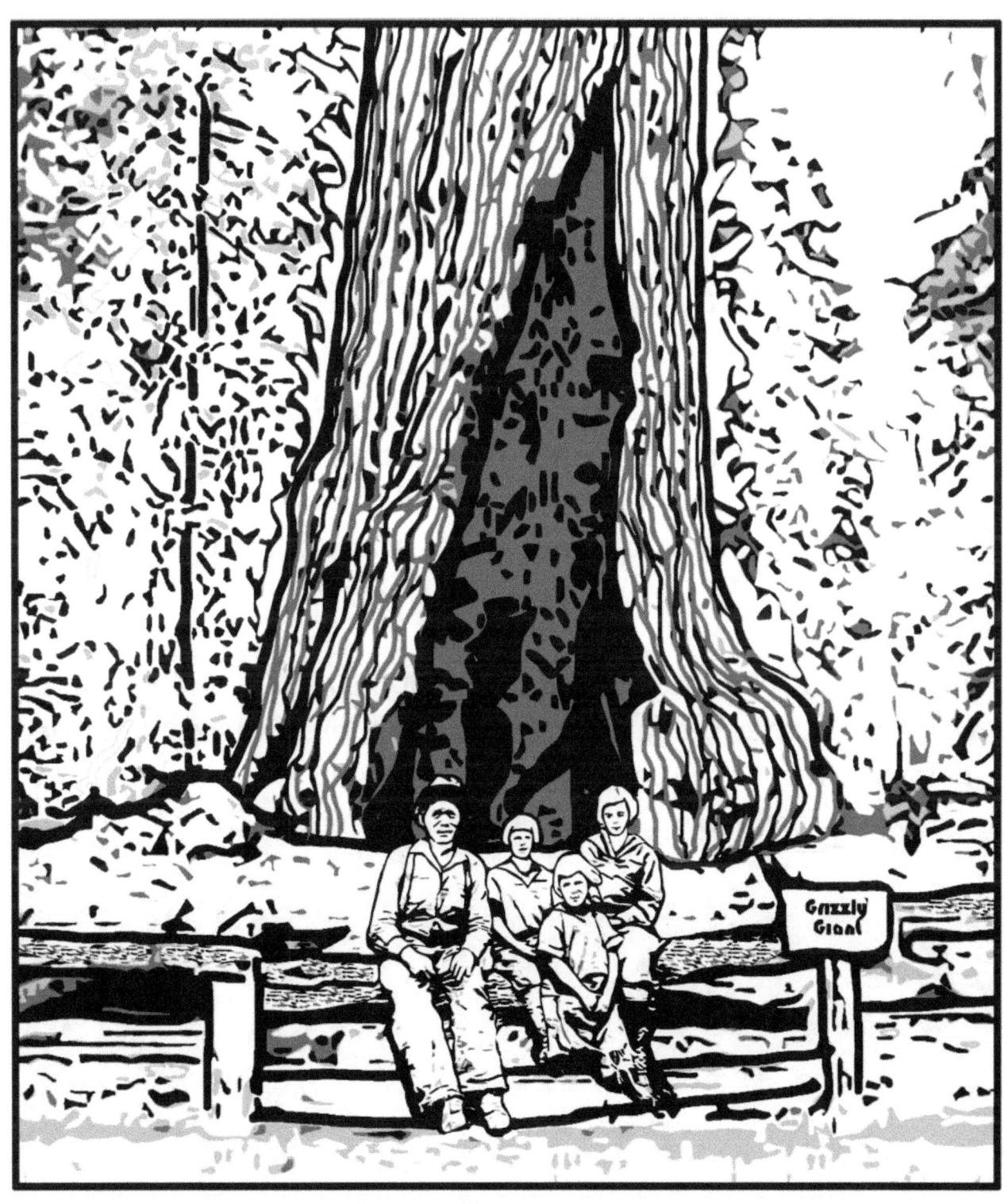

The Mariposa Grove in Yosemite National Park - 1920's

Balboa Park - San Diego

Balboa Park received land from the city of San Diego in 1868. Kate Sessions, a local business woman, agreed to plant 100 trees a year to beautify the park and to have a small place within the park to sell her plants. Many of the trees she planted are still there.

Work on the park progressed from 1903 to 1910. Balboa Park was named after the famous Spanish Explorer, Vasco Nunez de Balboa. Most of the park's historic buildings were built for the Panama - California Exposition in 1915.

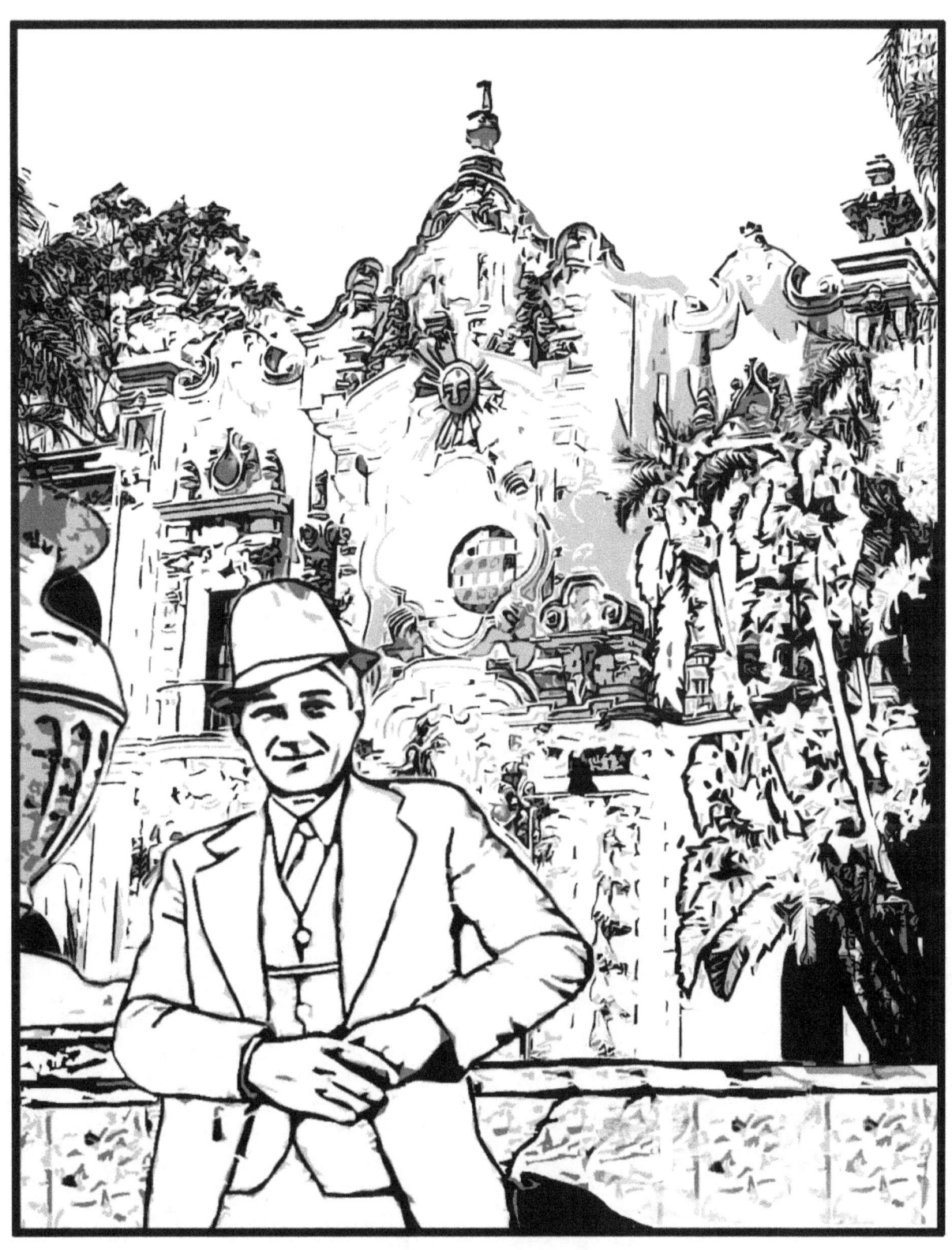

Balboa Park - 1934

The San Diego Zoo

The idea for a zoo in San Diego began with a gentleman named Harry Wegeforth in 1916. He started with a few animals in cages. In 1921, the Park Commission gave 50 acres of land to the zoo in Balboa Park. The grand opening of the zoo took place in 1923. Today, it is one of the world's finest zoos.

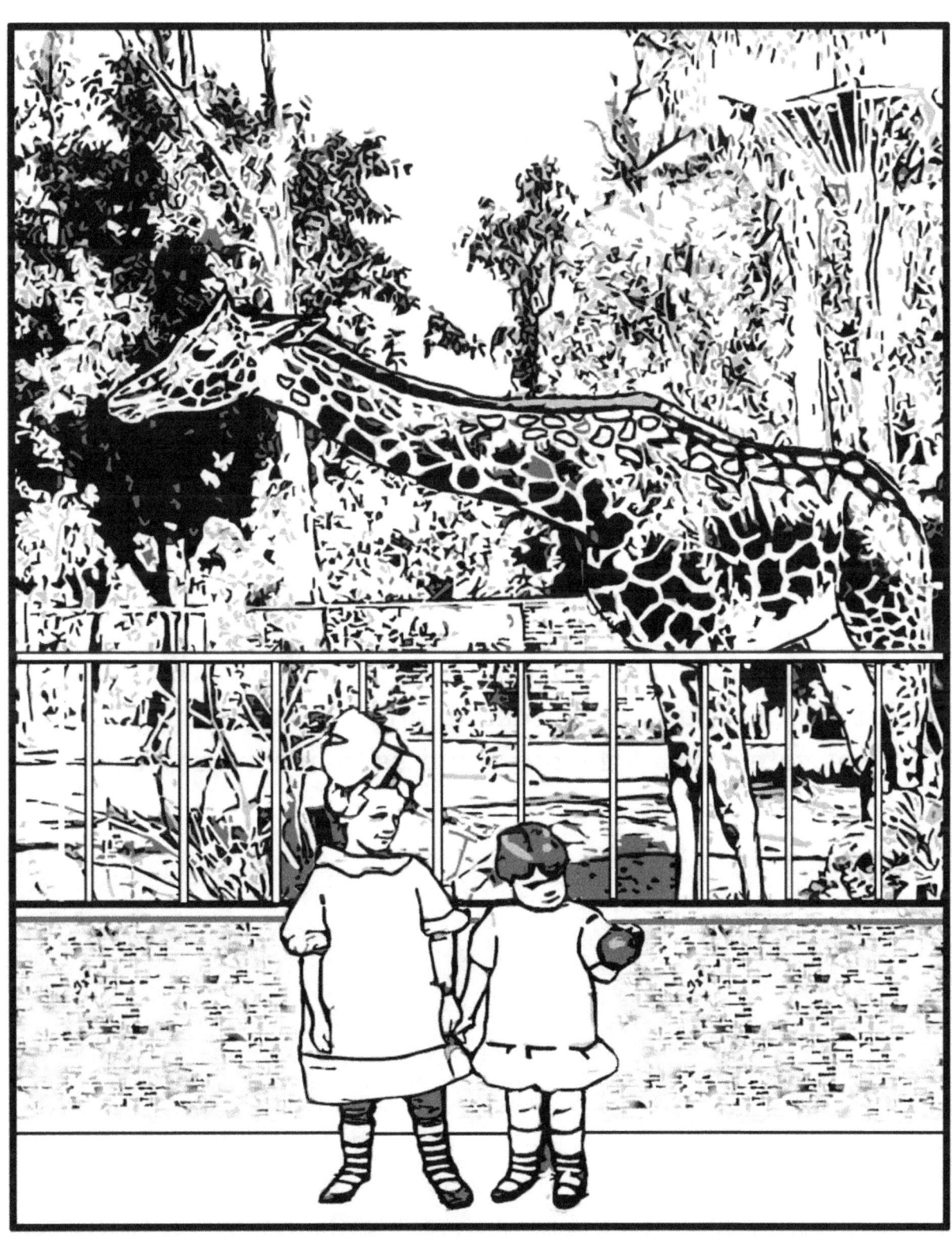

The San Diego Zoo - abt. 1924

La Jolla, California

La Jolla, California is the home of the famous Scripps Institution of Oceanography. It is known for its lovely beaches and dramatic coastline. It first became a major tourist attraction in the 1920's through the 1930's.

Today, it is still a haven for tourists from all over the country. With its year-round mild weather and lovely surroundings, it was voted one of the nicest places to live in the world.

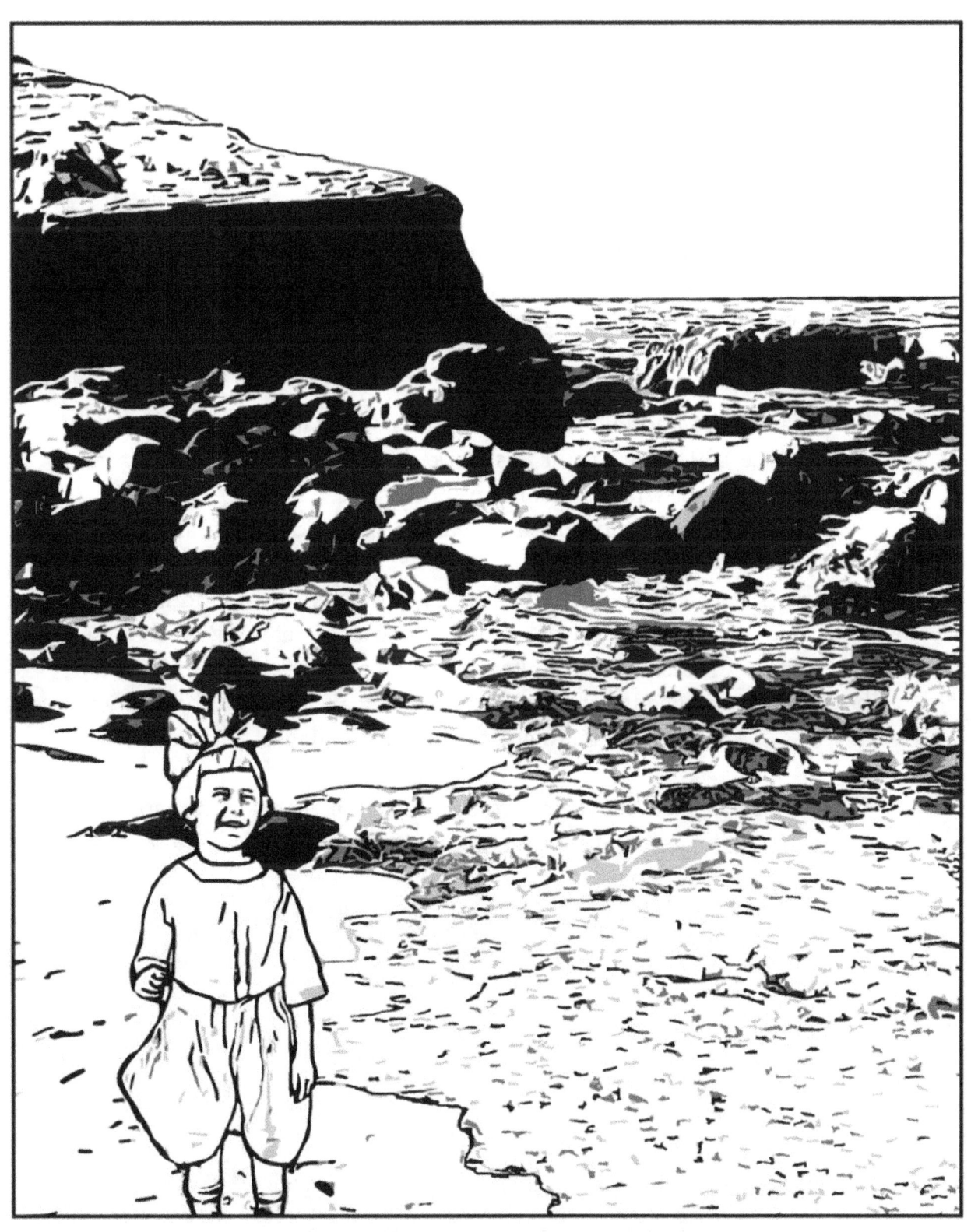

La Jolla, California beaches - abt. 1920

Author

The author, Carol Hill, was born in San Francisco, California. She attended the San Francisco Art Institute, the University of California, Davis, and graduated with a Bachelor of Arts degree in Graphic Communications from San Diego State University.

She has authored and illustrated numerous books including children's books. Since 1991, the author has worked as an Activities Director in retirement homes with independent and assisted living residents in Minnesota and Florida and is currently working in Utah.

This book tells a visual history of well known historical landmarks in San Francisco and on the California coast. A majority of the pictures in this book are taken from the author's own family photographs and used with photos of her own and those of her sister, Patty Arnett, to create these art collages.

The author has used her talents to develop coloring art that inspires creativity in all who use her books.